MW01077440

"In a world that's constantly shifting, *The Creative Way Forward* offers a timely and essential message: embrace change as an opportunity for growth and creativity. Martin's well-researched and thoughtfully crafted book provides a road map for staying resilient, adaptable, and true to yourself in the face of life's challenges."

—Daniel H. Pink, #1 *New York Times* best-selling author of *The Power of Regret* and *Drive*

"For those who struggle with change, Martin assures you that you are not alone and shows you how to embrace uncertainty. This compact guidebook has a bit of everything—compelling research, memorable anecdotes, practical tips, and easy-to-follow exercises—wrapped up in Martin's own relatable, personal narrative. It's my new go-to recommendation for personal change management."

—Julie Pham, PhD, CEO of CuriosityBased and author of *7 Forms of Respect*

"Change is uncomfortable, even change for the better. *The Creative Way Forward* shows you how to navigate change with the courage, curiosity, and creativity needed to unleash its possibilities and create a far more rewarding life."

—Dr. Margie Warrell, keynote speaker and best-selling author of *You've Got This!*

"Jen Martin masterfully provides a practical road map to navigate life's constant changes with creativity and resilience. This book is essential reading for anyone facing personal or professional transitions, offering insightful practices and tools that help harness the power of creativity in uncertain times. Martin's engaging writing and real-world examples inspire readers to embrace change as an opportunity for growth. Whether you're an individual looking to reinvent yourself or a leader steering through organizational shifts, this guide is a beacon of clarity and empowerment."

—Dr. Marshall Goldsmith, *New York Times* best-selling author of *The Earned Life, Triggers,* and *What Got You Here Won't Get You There*

"It's not easy navigating life's curveballs. Jen Martin's book is a helpful aid in these transitions, offering up a set of practices and tools that can build your creativity, resilience, and purpose. A must-read for uncertain times."

—Dr. Maya Shankar, cognitive scientist and host of the award-winning podcast *A Slight Change of Plans*

"*The Creative Way Forward* is an invaluable guide for today's constantly changing world. Well-researched, practical, and inspiring—it's a book you'll keep returning to again and again."

—Lindsey Pollak, *New York Times* best-selling author of *Recalculating: Navigate Your Career Through the Changing World of Work*

JEN MARTIN

THE
CREATIVE
WAY
FORWARD

A GUIDE FOR
NAVIGATING CHANGE
IN WORK AND LIFE

FAST
COMPANY
Press

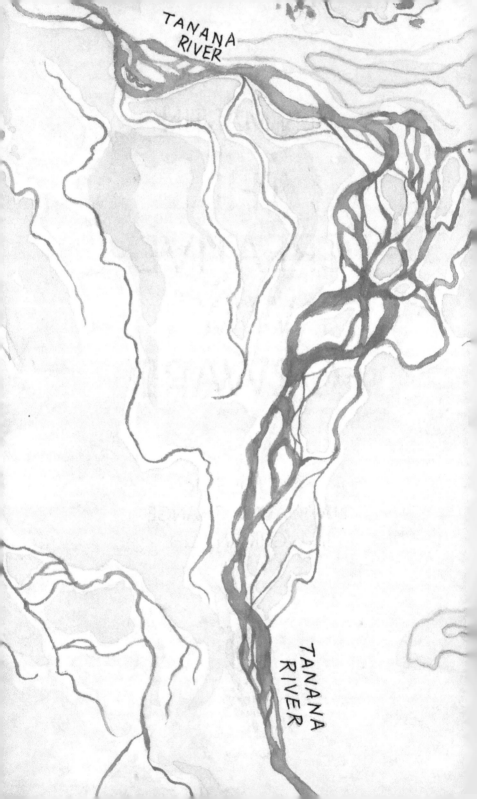

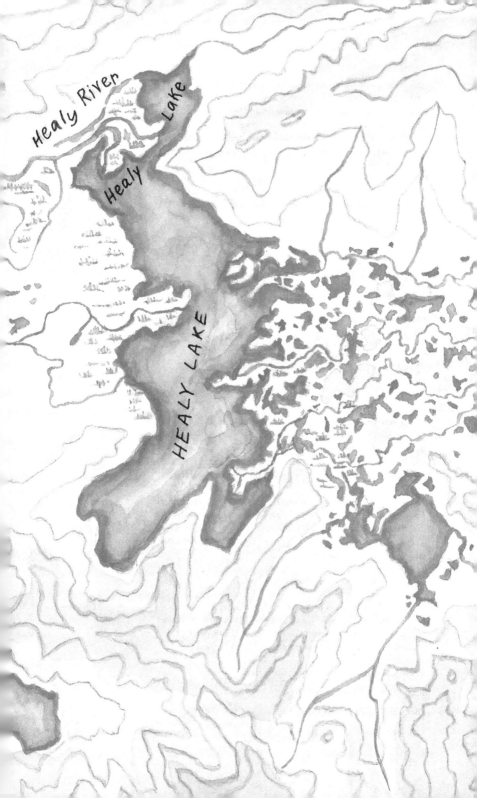

Fast Company Press
New York, New York
www.fastcompanypress.com

This work is being published under the Fast Company Press imprint by an exclusive arrangement with Fast Company. Fast Company and the Fast Company logo are registered trademarks of Mansueto Ventures, LLC. The Fast Company Press logo is a wholly owned trademark of Mansueto Ventures, LLC.

Distributed by River Grove Books

Design and composition by Greenleaf Book Group
Cover design by Greenleaf Book Group and John van der Woude
Cover photography by Jessica Cherry (Tanana Flats, Alaska)
Tanana River and Healy Lake painting by Gina Hoppner

Publisher's Cataloging-in-Publication data is available.

Print ISBN: 978-1-63908-108-0

eBook ISBN: 978-1-63908-109-7

First Edition

For Jackie and Ian

To exist is to change;
to change is to mature;
to mature is to go on
creating oneself endlessly.

—HENRI BERGSON

CONTENTS

INTRODUCTION

The river moves, but it follows a path.
When it tires of one journey, it rubs
through some rock to forge a new way.
Hard work, but that's its nature.

—KEKLA MAGOON

The Tanana River in Alaska winds almost six hundred miles from near the Canadian border, past the city of Fairbanks (where I was born and raised), to eventually join the Yukon River in the middle of the state. The Tanana is full of winding channels caused by flowing silt and debris washed down from mountain glaciers. These channels change unpredictably throughout the year, and in the spring and summer, when the river is the most erratic and full of silt, sometimes hourly. The shifting silt not only determines where a boat can pass through, but it also makes the water murky, creating an opaque and intimidating waterway.

When I was growing up, my family would travel by boat down the Tanana most summers to spend a week or two at our cabin on Healy Lake in a remote part of Alaska. The boat ride was definitely an experience. I remember how we would cram ourselves and all our gear into the sixteen-foot aluminum river boat, which had an outboard motor in back and bench seats with spaces in between for our bags, coolers, and excited dogs. The boat was uncovered, so we were at the mercy of the weather, getting drenched if it happened to be raining. I also remember not wanting to sit too close to the edge of the boat. If you fell into the river, there was a good chance you wouldn't make it out again, given the frigid water and the heavy silt that would rapidly fill your clothes, pulling you under.

Years later, when I asked my dad how he learned to navigate the river, he said it was trial and error. He would follow the flowing water while avoiding the ripples and swirls that told him something—a rock, a tree branch—was hidden below. Sometimes he would miscalculate the direction of a channel and end up ruining a motor prop on a gravel bar, but even that he saw as part of his learning process.

He said he didn't mind the river, but navigating it required him to simultaneously focus his attention on the channels emerging and shifting right in front of the boat and be aware of what was happening all around us, such as a log floating by or another boat headed in our direction. As he chose the next channel and moved the boat into it, new channels would become visible, merging in and out of one another, ending and starting unpredictably as he improvised forward.

Navigating the River of Change

It has been many years since I was last on the Tanana River, but as I was researching and writing this book, I realized it's a great metaphor for navigating change. We're all trying to find our way forward in constantly shifting and unpredictable conditions.

It seems like every day, there's an event or report telling us how uncertain the future is, from technology that will completely alter the way we live and work to rapid climate change that threatens our very existence. We are also dealing with changes at the personal level, whether planned or unexpected, such as switching jobs, ending a relationship, starting a family, or moving across the country, just to name a few.

People respond to change in different ways—sometimes avoiding it, sometimes embracing it—but I can't think of anyone who is fond of disruptions that come out of nowhere, upending carefully laid plans. However, it's important to not only get used to that kind of instability but also to learn how to navigate it well—because if there's one thing we can plan on, it's that nothing will stay the same.

In his book *21 Lessons for the 21st Century*, historian and author Yuval Noah Harari writes, "If you try to hold on to some stable identity, job, or worldview, you risk being left behind as the world flies by you with a whoosh. . . . To keep up with the world of 2050, you will need not merely to invent new ideas and products but above all to reinvent yourself again and again."

In other words, we have to be prepared to constantly adapt in big and small ways. Like my dad navigating the Tanana River, we have to be open to the messiness of trial-and-error learning. We need to focus on what's happening right here and now while also paying attention to what's around us and what's emerging ahead. And we need to be willing to let go again and again of what we've known and who we've been in order to follow the new route that just appeared, even when we're not sure where it will go.

Most of all, we need to be creative.

When people hear the word "creativity," they often associate it with the arts, such as painting a mural or writing a poem. However, its application is much wider. Creativity, broadly speaking, is the ability to create something new and useful from whatever is available. When you are navigating change, being creative means being able to work with whatever shows up and improvise along the way.

Being creative is not a "nice to have"; it's a necessity given not only the wide-ranging disruptions of today but also the unknown ones ahead. In fact, global surveys of leaders have ranked creativity as one of the top skills needed as we move into an uncertain future, with the majority of one survey's fifteen hundred respondents saying it's the most important.

The challenge is that in times of disruption—when we most need to be creative—we're often reactive since change and uncertainty can cause stress and fear. When we are reactive, our instinct is to protect ourselves. We focus on threats instead of possibilities, hanging on tight to the comfort of what we've known instead of being open to what's next.

There are plenty of reasons to be reactive: the problems for the planet, in society, and in our personal lives are very real. But we won't solve those problems when we are reactive. We need to access our creativity to come up with solutions and see other potential routes, particularly when everything keeps shifting.

While all of us can build our capacity to be creative, even during the most stressful times, it takes intention. An important part of your creative capacity comes from your mind and how you view yourself and the world around you. Since your mind is malleable, you can shape it in ways that support your adaptiveness or that keep you stuck. In this book, you'll learn how to develop your creative mind to support you through the twists and turns of change.

For more than a decade, I've been coaching and training individuals and teams to access their most creative selves, especially during transitions. I've had the privilege of working with a broad range of clients, from small nonprofits and start-ups to global companies and government agencies, as well as individuals reimagining their lives and careers. In the course of my work with others, as well as in my own life experiences and years of studying diverse fields such as psychology, adult development, neuroscience, and complexity science, I've distilled seven key practices to help people be creative as they navigate the river of change.

The Seven Practices for Navigating Change

The Greek philosopher Heraclitus reflected some twenty-five hundred years ago that you can't step into the same river twice. This famous quote is a great reminder that everything is always changing, even if it looks the same on the surface. Creativity is also not constant. You can be creative in one moment and not in another. It's easy to get overwhelmed, distracted, and discouraged. That's why you can't learn how to be creative just once and assume that you will stay creative through all the ups and downs of your journey. Constant practice is necessary to build your creative capacity, as well as your capacity to recover quickly when you slip into a reactive state.

The seven practices in this book are designed to help you do that. I call them "practices" because they are behaviors and perspectives that need to be repeated so they become habits, especially under stress. Think of them as exercises for the mind. Just as you can't expect to do physical exercise once and stay fit, you need to keep doing these practices to train and sustain your creative mind. And the more transitions you traverse using these practices, the better equipped you'll be to handle the next unexpected event.

Each chapter features one practice along with the research and science behind why it works. The chapters also include stories, examples, and tools for putting the practices into action. At the end of each chapter are reflection questions to help you think more about the concepts in the chapter and apply them to your life and work situations. Grab a journal and jot down your thoughts as you read through these questions (or set aside time to do this later). The time spent reflecting on these questions is well worth it since reflecting on what you've read will help you recall the information later when you need it.

This book is designed to be a guidebook for navigating change, and the practices and tools are the essential items you'll need as you travel on your journey. On a journey, you pack what you might need, but you don't use every item at once. Likewise, you'll always have the practices and tools from this book with you, but you may use some more than others as you learn which ones work for you in different situations.

Whether you're making your way through a personal or professional transition or you just want to be more creative in the midst of constant change, this book will show you the way forward. Let's get started.

1

EXPECT A JOURNEY

*The journey, not
the destination matters.*

—T. S. ELIOT

The hotel meeting room in San Diego, California, was abuzz as retreat attendees arrived and took seats in the chairs arranged in a large circle. The energy in the room was palpable—a mix of excitement, jet lag, curiosity, and likely some apprehension. These nineteen leaders had signed up for a ten-month program on leading change in their organizations and communities, and this was their first in-person event.

My co-facilitators and I had spent months designing this program, and we were excited to get started. The participants were just as eager to start work on their plans for the future. But we asked them first to reflect on the past:

- *What important transitions helped you become who you are today?*

- *What challenges did you navigate?*

- *What did you learn?*

These are questions we don't often ask ourselves, yet they make us stop and think. We learn and grow not when we're in constant action but when we take time to reflect on our experiences. Thinking about changes we've already been through lets us absorb the lessons learned and prepares us for the next disruption, whether that's in our organization, our career, or our personal life.

To help the leaders in that kickoff retreat reflect on these questions, we asked them to create "journey maps," putting down on paper the key milestones, turning points, and transitions that helped shape who they had become. Everyone approached their map a little differently: Some drew elaborate and detailed pathways while others were more matter-of-fact, listing bullet points and brief descriptions.

After sharing their maps in small groups, the participants taped them up on the walls so we could see them all together. I remember the curiosity and conversations in the room as people wandered around getting a peek into each other's lives beyond job titles and roles. It quickly became clear that every person had been on a *journey*. Collectively, the maps showed high points and achievements as well as low points and unplanned detours. While individual experiences were different, the shared maps generated a feeling of connection within the group. These leaders realized they were not alone—that the nonlinear shape of their own journey was more the norm than an outlier.

One retreat participant told me later that her habit had been to set a goal, follow a plan to reach it, and if she didn't make that goal or hit a certain level of success, assume she had failed. But as she reflected on her journey map over time, she realized that many of the things she's most grateful for in her career and life weren't planned. Since then, she has tried to stay open to whatever lies ahead: "You can get stuck in thinking it has to go a certain way, but that's really limiting. It's *always* a journey."

Map Your Journey

On a large sheet of paper, draw your journey, highlighting key milestones, turning points, and transitions. Make it as elaborate or as simple as you like, but try to include at least five points in time or experiences across your life that have shaped who you are today.

Once you've created your map, reflect on the following questions:

- What helped you through those transitions?
- What lessons did you learn from those experiences?
- How did those transitions provide opportunities for your growth and development?

For a downloadable version of this tool, visit tools.thecreativewayforward.com

Journeys Are Full of Curves

Our journeys are full of ups and downs, endings and beginnings, not just because unexpected disruptions come our way but also  because that's the rhythm of life and nature. Every living system, whether a plant, a person, an organization, or a community, moves through a natural pattern of growth and decline. This pattern, when mapped on a graph, forms a sigmoid curve, or "S-curve," which looks like a stretched-out letter *S*.

In the mid-1990s, Charles Handy, a management consultant and fellow at the London Business School, applied the S-curve concept to the developmental processes of both people and institutions. He observed that for continued growth, neither individuals nor organizations can stay on one S-curve; they need to move along multiple S-curves across their lifespans, renewing or reinventing themselves in order to thrive under new and evolving conditions.

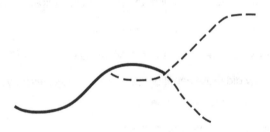

However, Handy also noted a paradox: When things are going well, people naturally assume they should keep doing what they're doing. But that's exactly when they should be thinking about what's next. He said, "The secret to constant growth is to start a new sigmoid curve before the first one peters out . . . to get the new curve through its initial explorations and floundering before the first curve begins to dip downward."

Since we can't predict when the curve we're currently on will start to decline or even abruptly end, we need to stay curious and be ready to switch course. If we get stuck in wanting safety and control or hang on too long to what we've done and who we've been, we miss the cues telling us to shift. And if we wait until the need for change is very clear (or we're forced to make a change), the change can be harder to pull off because in crisis mode, time, resources, and energy are often in low supply.

What we can expect is that with every significant change—the company restructure, the relationship end, the health problem, the retirement—we also go through an internal transition as we integrate the new reality into our life. This transition isn't like a simple flip of a TV channel. It's a process. And it's been mapped.

The Internal Experience of Change

Elisabeth sat across the desk from the medical director at Columbia University Medical Center, preparing herself to speak. Although she had toyed with the idea of not sharing her news with him, she knew she had no choice. She was pregnant, which meant she had to give up her coveted pediatric residency. It was 1958, and there were no exceptions to Columbia's rule, even for someone as talented and hardworking as Elisabeth. The medical director was disappointed to disqualify her and offered to hold a spot for her the following year, but that didn't change her current situation.

While excited to become a mom, Elisabeth was also anxious about her career. Trained as a physician in her native Switzerland, she had moved to the United States to start a new life with her husband, who was also a resident doctor. She knew his income wouldn't cover expenses for the two of them, let alone three. She needed to find another residency.

The options were slim since most residencies in New York City were already filled, but in time, Elisabeth heard about an opening in the psychiatric ward at Manhattan State Hospital. Psychiatry was last on her list of specialty interests, but she needed a job, and they were willing to hire her. She accepted the position.

Although Elisabeth had to let go of her original plan, this unexpected detour led her to an extraordinary career. Elisabeth Kübler-Ross became a globally recognized pioneer in end-of-life care and counseling. In her role as a hospital psychiatrist in the 1960s, Elisabeth was shocked that very few doctors or patients would talk openly about death, even when the patient was terminal. Wanting to help people face rather than avoid their final transition, she started interviewing patients and training medical students. In her 1969 book, *On Death and Dying*, Elisabeth shares five stages she observed many people go through: denial, anger, bargaining, depression, and acceptance. While these stages were initially about processing the end of life, Elisabeth believed this information could also be useful for people going through any kind of change, since all transitions are about loss, acceptance, and moving into what's next.

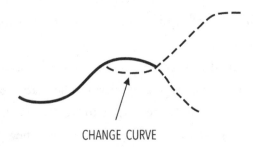

CHANGE CURVE

Dr. Kübler-Ross gave us a general map of the internal experience of change. Over time, it has been expanded upon and become known as the Change Curve. While there is no perfect model that can account for every person's unique experience, the Change Curve describes what transitions might be like, which is helpful in preparing for them. Building on Dr. Kübler-Ross's insights and the work of many others, I've developed my own version of the Change Curve. It summarizes the internal processing of change and includes four parts:

- **Struggle:** not yet accepting what has happened or is going to happen

- **Regroup:** having accepted the change that is happening, reassessing what's most important

- **Explore:** imagining and testing possible directions

- **Commit:** actively working toward a new direction

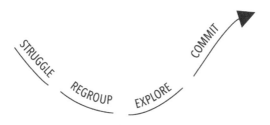

While I present these four in what looks like a linear sequence, a transition is rarely that simplistic. No two people will move through the Change Curve the same way, and the same person may go through it differently during different transitions. For example, if you just lost your job, you might go through *Struggle* before you can figure out what's next, or you might go right to *Explore* while you are also processing your loss. Or if you're thinking about moving to a new city or town, you might start off in *Explore* as you imagine and visit different places but later find yourself in *Struggle* when it's time to leave and let go of your old life.

Rather than thinking of these four as phases or stages, which implies linear progress from one to the next, consider them as four points on a map that you may visit for varying amounts of time depending on your situation and the transition you're navigating.

STRUGGLE

Struggle describes the point during a transition where we haven't yet accepted what is happening or is about to happen. We may be in denial or angry or reactively trying to "fix things" to avoid the change. We may not be aware of what we're feeling, or we may be experiencing various emotions but trying to ignore them, possibly out of fear of what they're telling us. But the only way out of Struggle is *through it*, acknowledging what's happening and letting go of what's ending.

Before I started my own business in my early forties, I went through a long, drawn-out process of Struggle. I would repeatedly make the decision to quit my job and go off on my own. Then I would talk myself out of it, coming up with all the reasons why it wasn't the right time. Fear of failing was a big deterrent, but letting go of what I had was even bigger. Only when I came to terms with leaving an organization I loved and losing the security and identity it provided was I able to take the leap and move forward.

Although people don't like to think or talk about loss, it is inevitable with any change. Even good changes like getting married or being promoted at work involve letting go of something. We feel the pain of the loss more than the joy of whatever is gained. That pain keeps us focused on trying to preserve what we have now. To move out of Struggle takes awareness and intentionality, and it may take longer than we expect or want.

In 2000, elders of the Hopi Nation gathered in Oraibi, Arizona, and shared a message with the world about living in the new millennium. The following excerpt is helpful to remember when you find yourself trying to hold onto a situation, a job, or a relationship, for example, even as it's rapidly changing:

> Here is a river flowing now very fast. It is so great and swift that there are those who will be afraid, who will try to hold on to the shore. They are being torn apart and will suffer greatly. . . . The elders say we must let go of the shore. Push off into the middle of the river, and keep our heads above water. . . . We are to take nothing personally, least of all ourselves, for the moment we do, our spiritual growth and journey come to a halt.

REGROUP

Once we've accepted the change that is happening, we Regroup, reflecting on where we are right now and assessing what's most important. Things aren't figured out yet, and you may still be letting go of aspects of your old life or who you have been. It may feel like you're operating in parallel universes—outwardly moving forward to meet new demands and take on responsibilities while inwardly feeling as if in a blank space, suspended in time. You may be tired, run-down, and unfocused. You may need more time alone.

It may seem like nothing is happening in Regroup, but it is actually a creative period. A common metaphor for this point in a transition is a caterpillar turning into a butterfly. The caterpillar wraps itself into a cocoon and then dissolves into the equivalent of caterpillar soup. What's happening during this period of apparent nothingness—no longer a caterpillar, not yet a butterfly—is, in fact, pretty amazing. Even though nothing has taken form yet, the caterpillar's imaginal cells are starting to reassemble what used to be the caterpillar into the butterfly's wings, body, and legs.

Similarly, during Regroup, we're in an in-between state, dissolving our old identity and preparing ourselves for what we'll become. While you may want to skip this uncomfortable point in the Change Curve, you need to stay in the messiness long enough to disrupt old patterns. Most of us have been socialized to rush to fix problems and fill gaps, and yes, in a crisis, you need to act quickly. But when that quick-fix approach is your default, you are likely to rely on what's familiar or has worked in the past rather than staying open to something new.

One of my clients came up with a great analogy for the need to slow down during Regroup. When she was going through a high-stress transition, she remembered her father, a boater, talking about steering his boat through "pea soup"—the heavy marine fog in which visibility is so low that you risk running aground or into other boats unless you reduce speed. This metaphor helped her pause and pay attention to what was emerging even when she wanted to hurry up and make rapid-fire decisions.

Ironically, to meet the fast pace of today's world and, likely, the world of the future, we have to slow down. This doesn't mean letting go of responsibilities and spending weeks alone in a cabin (though that might sound tempting). It does mean prioritizing your time to create pockets of "blank space" for renewal and reflection. To find that extra time, ask yourself the following:

- *What must I absolutely do right now?*
- *What can I let go of, say no to, scale back, or temporarily slow down?*

Then, schedule time in your calendar—maybe it's thirty minutes every day, an hour a week, or a weekend a month that's just for you.

Regroup is not wasted time. It's essential for creatively approaching your future.

EXPLORE

Explore is the point where we shift our attention to what's possible, imagining alternate futures and testing potential directions. I love to ask clients who are at this point, "What's possible now that wasn't before?"

There are a few things to keep in mind while in Explore. First, be selective about who you share your ideas with, since sometimes other people's response to a new idea is to state all the reasons it might not work. Not everyone closest to you will be your biggest supporter at this point, especially if the change you're considering will affect them.

Second, don't close out an idea too soon yourself. Large companies have departments dedicated to research and development exactly for this reason: so employees have the freedom to explore new directions and incubate ideas before they are tested. Create your own R&D space during Explore.

Finally, be aware that as you explore new directions, your innate need for certainty and safety can send you looping back through Struggle and Regroup. I call this the Transition Eddy. Like the skillful paddling needed to move a raft out of the swirl of an eddy in a river, intentional effort is required to exit a Transition Eddy.

In a Transition Eddy, we may find ourselves repeating old patterns, ruminating on a mix of emotions, or getting sidetracked. Self-doubt can show up because we're trying to move into something we haven't yet mastered, let alone experienced. We may compare ourselves to others who appear to be ahead of us, which can dampen our creativity and throw us into the dark circling waters of rethinking, doubting, or procrastinating.

A Transition Eddy can be useful if you need time to reconsider an idea or process emotions that need to be cleared before you can move forward. But if you find yourself looping again and again, you may need to make some bold decisions to get yourself out of the swirl and into the flow of the river.

The iterative nature of exploring requires patience and an ongoing assessment of whether the opportunities that present themselves are aligned with your values and strengths. The risk at this point is to take on too much too soon. I've seen many people (including myself) become overwhelmed when trying to sort through multiple options or do too many things at once. For example, looking back at my most recent Explore period, I was running my consulting and coaching business, exploring a product business with a friend, planning a podcast, teaching college courses, participating in a marketing program, and working with an editor on this book—all while trying to raise a family and live my life. It was too much, and the weight of it all sapped my creative energy. I had to strip it back to my client work, the book, and my family and be more intentional in my choices. I learned (again) how important it is to prioritize during Explore, testing only a few options at a time.

There is an art to navigating change, especially at this point in the Change Curve. If you choose a path forward too early, you may force a decision prematurely. If you wait for perfection, a great opportunity may pass you by. Regardless, at some point, you'll need to commit to a direction.

COMMIT

Commit is the point on the Change Curve where we focus on a new direction and actively work toward it, entering the next S-curve. That might sound easy compared to the challenges of the other three points, but committing can be the most difficult point in a transition because it means letting go of other possible routes and taking a risk that may or may not work out. It can be tempting to stay in Explore, keeping your options open and waiting. But if you go too long without a new direction to pour your energy into, that energy is spent instead on rethinking the right next step. I see this in my clients and in myself when there is hesitation to commit. We second-guess the direction again and again: *Is it the best choice, or will I regret it later?*

There's a quote taped to my office wall from the Scottish mountaineer and writer W. H. Murray: "Until one is committed there is hesitancy, the chance to draw back, always ineffectiveness. Concerning all acts of initiative (and creation), there is one elementary truth, the ignorance of which kills countless ideas and splendid plans: that the moment one definitely commits oneself, then Providence moves too. All sorts of things occur to help one that would never otherwise have occurred."

You have likely experienced this yourself at some point. Once you committed—made a decision and began to take action—opportunities and supportive people started to show up just when you needed them, as if the universe was trying to help you along. You probably also felt the inspiration and energy spark when there was a compelling vision to work toward. This doesn't mean everything turned out as planned, but you were in motion, and that momentum propelled you forward.

Committing to what's next is not necessarily a singular, monumental decision (though it can be). More likely, it's a series of smaller decisions and actions. Like my dad choosing a channel in the Tanana River, moving our boat into it, and then watching for the next one, you need to pick a path and then keep moving, knowing the next path will show up at some point along the way.

Wanting to choose the "right" direction is deeply ingrained, but there is no one right way. What looks like the perfect option can become unbearable, and what seems like a terrible situation may hold opportunities that cannot otherwise be accessed. You can see only so far ahead. So pick a vision you want to work toward, commit to it, and then stay flexible, since you may need to change course again (something we'll look at more in chapter seven).

Reflect on the Change Curve

If you are currently in a transition, identify where you are on the Change Curve. Given what you know about that point on the Change Curve, what action or attitude would be most helpful to you right now?

The Change Curve, like any map, cannot account for everything you'll experience during a transition. As the philosopher Alfred Korzybski says, "A map is not the territory it represents, but, if correct, it has a similar structure to the territory, which accounts for its usefulness." What the Change Curve does provide is a tool for reflection, an opportunity to step out of your experience to think about what is happening and what you might need right now. It can orient you if you are feeling lost, and it reminds you that ups and downs are part of the journey—that whatever is happening right now won't last forever.

The Big Picture

If you look at an aerial photo of the Tanana River, you can see the river's many winding curves and how it moves around sandbars and splits into multiple routes as it makes its way across Alaska. If you could get an aerial view of your life, you would see how it too is full of S-curves and the Change Curves that bridge between them. In fact, it's estimated that people spend almost half their adult lives navigating big transitions, the kind that require them to grow into their next selves and into the next S-curve. It's a long journey, though, and making your way through each of those Change Curves can take longer than you might expect—often several years. While a Change Curve is more evident during a significant change, even mundane disruptions, such as switching to a new gym or learning a new timesheet tracking system, can cause you to go through a mini–Change Curve.

With the right mapping tool, you could also see how multiple layers of change are occurring at any given time. Think about your life right now. You may be going through changes at work and also in your personal life even as broader shifts are happening in your community and country and on the planet. Even if you're not aware of the many changes going on at once, they influence you just the same.

From this big-picture perspective, it's clear that our lives are not stable with periodic transitions. They are in transition with periods of stability (and those stable times may seem more and more fleeting). We may think stability is what we're after, but what we really need is to keep building our capacity to constantly adapt. We need to keep reminding ourselves that disruption is the norm and that, many times, we'll pursue directions we think will work out that don't. New opportunities and new challenges will show up, taking us in directions we couldn't have planned. Prior routes we thought were gone may reappear when we're better prepared to pursue them. No matter what happens, when we expect a journey, we're better prepared for the inevitable twists and turns ahead.

FOR REFLECTION

- Do you tend to expect a journey or to expect stability? How do you know?

- How does your expectation change your experience?

- Think about your last work or life transition (one that is already completed). What did you learn from it that you want to remember for your next Change Curve?

2

BE PRESENT

*Be still like a mountain, and flow
like a great river.*

—LAO TZU

My family's trip to the cabin on Healy Lake each year took a lot of advance preparation, with many lists made and stores visited to ensure we had everything we'd need. When it was time to leave, we would load up the truck with all our supplies and drive more than one hundred miles from our house in Fairbanks to the Tanana River.

Launching the boat was always a process—transferring stuff from the truck, getting the boat into the water, arguing about who had forgotten what—but eventually we would be ready to go. Dad would hold the boat steady as the rest of us clambered in, and then he would get in, push off from the shore, and quickly move to the back of the boat to start the motor. As he maneuvered the boat to find the channels, he avoided the riverbanks because of the sweepers—fallen trees reaching over the water that could trap a boat. While there are many dangers on fast-flowing rivers like the Tanana, sweepers are particularly tricky. If you don't pay attention, you can find yourself tangled up in one.

When I think about navigating change, I remember those sweepers. They are a great metaphor for the distractions—like worrying about the future or ruminating on the past—that can keep us trapped in reactive thinking. And we're more susceptible to reactive thinking when we're not paying attention to the present moment.

According to research, we spend almost half our waking hours with our mind wandering all over the place. While intentionally letting the mind wander can be a tool for coming up with creative ideas (which we'll look at in chapter seven), many people spend way too much time distracted, not focused on what they're doing and experiencing right now. They're thinking about what to make for dinner while reading an email, going through their mental to-do list in the middle of a meeting, or trying to remember whether they closed the garage door while having coffee with a friend.

In this distracted state, we're more likely to become anxious or have negative thoughts in stressful situations. Instead of figuring out what to do next, we may ruminate on what we've done wrong or worry about all the terrible things that might happen. We're no longer in the flow of the river; we're stuck in the sweepers. And the more often we get stuck, the more it becomes a habit—we're scattered and reactive instead of creatively moving forward.

What can help us avoid the mental sweepers?

The practice of being present.

When you are present, you notice what's happening around you without judgment. You're also aware of what's happening within you—your thoughts, feelings, and sensations—without being driven or snagged by it. This awareness creates a little space between whatever is happening right now and your response to it, giving you an opportunity to *choose* what you do next rather than simply react.

The practice of being present, or what's often called mindfulness, has been around for centuries in various forms. However, it's gotten more attention in recent years as numerous studies have shown how it can improve physical health, creativity, and mental flexibility, as well as reduce anxiety, stress, and negativity bias (the human tendency to focus on negatives more than positives). Opinions differ as to whether mindfulness and being present are distinct or the same. In this book, I treat them as one and use the term "being present." Regardless of what it's called, it's a powerful practice for navigating change. While all the practices in this book are important, if I were forced to choose one as foundational to the rest, this would be it.

Moving Forward by Being Present

Imagine for a moment that you are a firefighter. You're in tip-top shape, and, with years of experience under your belt, you trust your knowledge of what to do even under the unpredictable conditions of a forest fire, where a shift in the wind can change the situation in minutes. On this particular day, you and your crewmates parachute into Montana's remote wilderness to fight a fire. It seems like a textbook blaze that won't take long to contain.

Once on the ground, you and the other firefighters spend an hour gathering equipment and waiting for instructions on how best to get the fire under control. The foreman decides, however, that conditions have become too dangerous, and the crew must move out of the area. With the foreman in the lead, the group starts toward the river, but suddenly, the fire jumps the gulch that until now had separated it from you. The tall dry grass all around you will burn faster than the forest. You've never experienced a grassland fire, and when the foreman suddenly switches directions and leads the group up a steep ridge, you know something is very wrong.

The foreman then yells to drop your tools—the very tools, such as shovels and saws, critical for battling forest fires. In many ways, the tool you are carrying is an extension of you, part of your identity as a firefighter, so despite what he said, you instinctively hold on to your heavy saw as you push yourself even harder to get up the ridge to safety. The temperature is now above one hundred degrees Fahrenheit, and the sound of the swift-moving fire is deafening, as if a jumbo jet were bearing down on you. Safety is only two hundred yards away, but you won't get there if you don't drop that saw.

What would you do?

This is the situation that unfolded during the Mann Gulch Fire in the summer of 1949. Thirteen firefighters died. After being told to drop their tools, the majority didn't. The foreman and two men who did follow his order, dropping their tools early and running to safety, were the only survivors.

Tragically, since then, more firefighters have died in other fires because they didn't let go of their tools. What makes this even more heartbreaking are the follow-up studies showing they would have survived if they had.

This lesson applies not just to firefighters but to all of us. When a situation changes quickly, the heightened uncertainty can make us fearful, and we revert to a habitual response—very often without realizing it. It's hard to let go of what has worked in the past because there's comfort in familiarity. To let go of old ways and see a different route forward, we have to be present enough to realize that we're hanging on to nothing more than a habit.

During the Mann Gulch Fire, the foreman, Wag Dodge, evidently had that level of presence. Seeing that the situation had turned dire, he ordered his crew to drop their tools so they could run faster, but he soon realized the fire was coming so fast that they might not be able to outrun it. He had an idea.

He stopped, pulled out a match, and lit it, igniting the grass in front of him. As it quickly burst into flames and then burned out, he yelled to the others to join him and then lay down in the smoldering ashes and covered his face. No one joined him. They likely thought he was crazy to lie down rather than run. They hadn't yet learned about escape fires—fires started on purpose to burn up the fuel before the larger fire reaches it, creating a burned area that the larger blaze will skip over. Dodge said later he had come up with this counterintuitive idea in the moment.

Dodge was in a highly volatile, high-stress situation, yet he was able to be creative and adaptive—switching directions when conditions changed, giving his men the radical instruction to drop their tools, and ultimately coming up with an even more radical idea that saved his life and might have saved the lives of others.

While we may not find ourselves in situations that extreme, we too can be creative during challenging times by learning how to be present. Dr. Amishi Jha, a neuroscientist who researches the brain's ability to pay attention, has studied the effects of mindfulness training for firefighters and soldiers. She has found that when people who work in high-stress situations learn how to be mindful or present, their concentration, emotional regulation, and working memory increase. They become better at holding several options in mind at once while determining which is the best possible choice.

Being present enough to regulate our nervous system in the face of a challenge is not something humans naturally do. We have to learn it. That's because the brain's default when we perceive we are in danger is to cue the body to prepare for fight or flight or, if we feel overwhelmed enough, to freeze. In this reactive state, called the threat response, we have less access to our prefrontal cortex, the part of the brain critical for effective decision-making, future planning, and creative adaptation. This fast reactive response is useful when, for example, you're jumping out of the way of an oncoming car. It's less useful when the threat before you is a looming deadline or an unexpected change, such as a job loss or the end of a relationship. The same body chemistry is set in motion, and even though your life is not immediately at risk, it can feel like it is.

However, the capacity to be present is not developed during crisis situations. It needs to be practiced during the lesser challenges of day-to-day living so it becomes what we automatically access when it matters most. "It's like doing a core workout for your body," Dr. Jha explains. "If you've got core strength, it will help you in a variety of ways—you're going to be able to maneuver through many different physically strenuous circumstances. Those brain routes become more accustomed to turning on and will start to fire instinctively the more you practice."

Training yourself to be in the present moment is an ongoing practice. The tools in this chapter are designed to help you keep developing that muscle so you can recognize when your mind is distracted—trapped in a "sweeper"—and bring your attention back to what you're doing and feeling right now.* As you strengthen your ability to be in the present moment, you'll increase your capacity to find your way forward through even the most challenging times.

Meditate with Focused Attention or with Open Awareness

Dr. Amishi Jha's research shows that meditating just twelve minutes a day can improve attention and working memory. There are many ways to meditate and build the "muscle" of being present, but here are two meditations that I find helpful:

Focused Attention Meditation

Sit where you can be comfortable, and focus on your breath as it moves in and out of your body. If thoughts or other distractions pull your attention away, notice this without judgment, and then return your attention to your breath. Don't worry if your mind wanders; it will! The point of the meditation is the *refocusing* of your attention back to the breath.

Open Awareness Meditation

Rather than focusing on one thing, such as your breath, let your attention broaden. Be aware of what your senses pick up around you, as well as

continued

---

* Some people who have experienced trauma may find the tools in this chapter triggering and may need professional support to use them.

your thoughts and feelings as they come and go within you, without judgment. What sounds or scents do you notice? What's the temperature? Is the air moving around you? Just be present in the moment, and let everything flow by you without being attached to any of it.

The Power of Breath to Bring You Present

I used to find it patronizing when someone would say to me, "Take a deep breath." I would either take a quick breath or ignore the suggestion. After I dug into the research on breathing, however, I began to understand why breathing is so important (beyond keeping us alive). Studies show that intentional breathing is one of the fastest ways to feel calmer and become present with what is happening right now. It's now one of the first tools I turn to when I or my clients need help managing a stressful situation since breathing can override the body's stress reaction in ways that simply thinking "I need to calm down" cannot. But intentional breathing is more than just taking a breath; what's important is *how* you take that breath.

Breathing is one of the few body functions that are both consciously controlled (we can decide to take a deeper breath) and automatic (we keep breathing without thinking about it). When you're stressed or fearful, your breathing automatically becomes quick and shallow. When you notice this, you can choose to breathe deeply and slowly. That sends a message to the brain that there's no need to be on high alert right now. The exhale is particularly important because it activates the parasympathetic nervous system (the "rest and digest" system), which counterbalances the body's fight-flight-freeze reaction by slowing the heart rate.

Try it right now. Pause your reading and do one of the Breathe Intentionally exercises. Afterward, notice how you feel.

Breathe Intentionally

Four-Count Breathing

Used by the U.S. Navy SEALs, "box breathing" is four-count breathing that will help you feel present and focused. Here is how you do it:

- Completely exhale the air from your lungs.
- Hold your lungs empty for four counts.
- Inhale through your nose for four counts.
- When your lungs are full, hold for four counts.
- Then exhale through your nose for four counts (or try exhaling through your mouth, which I find easier).

Repeat this sequence three or four times. However, if you feel light-headed or out of breath, stop the exercise, and try again later with fewer counts.

Long-Exhale Breathing

- Take a deep inhale for four counts, filling your lungs.
- Hold your breath for a couple of seconds.
- Then exhale, letting the exhale be longer than the inhale (six to eight counts), completely emptying your lungs.
- Do this a couple more times. Then notice how you feel.

While I was writing this book, a long-time client shared with me how intentional breathing supported her through one of the most challenging periods of her life. One night a few years earlier, Natalie's then-sixteen-year-old daughter told her that she was having suicidal thoughts. Suddenly, Natalie said, her whole world shifted. She kicked into the crisis management mode so familiar from her twenty-plus years of working in government and social service agencies. She sat with her daughter all night and checked her into the local children's hospital the next morning. She made sure the hospital's best doctors were on the case, followed her daughter's progress multiple times daily with hospital staff, and arranged for psychiatrists and therapists as her daughter began to recover. But Natalie soon realized that in her efficiency, she was pushing away her own feelings. And by disconnecting from her own experience, she was less able to provide her daughter with the deeper emotional support she needed during that tough period.

"Up to that point, I had lived in my head," Natalie told me. "I was a great strategist, able to analyze problems and find solutions quickly. My default was to move, move, move. But what I didn't know was that was a way of protecting myself. . . . I wasn't really aware of what I was doing."

After exploring various mindfulness trainings, Natalie began a practice of sitting quietly for ten to twenty minutes in the morning and at night, focusing her mind on gratitude or compassion and paying attention to her heart rate and her breath. After a while, she noticed a difference—she felt calmer and got overwhelmed less often. When stressful events occurred, she was not snagged by them as easily, and when she was, she found she could quickly recover with intentional breathing.

"This wasn't something that happened overnight," Natalie said. "It took a long time. But I knew I had to do something different because my previous patterns of coping with stress weren't effective anymore."

Natalie's practice helped her to be more present and to provide the kind of support her daughter and family needed. "I have been practicing these techniques for more than two years now," she added, "and I absolutely feel like I have created more expansiveness within me. It creates an inner pause. In that pause, you can become aware that you have a choice of how you want to respond. That new choice can change the trajectory of the moment and the outcome."

Being Present through Body Awareness

One of the most direct ways to become present is to notice and connect with your body. However, many of us spend a lot of time in our head, almost forgetting we have a body—or, as the late Sir Ken Robinson joked during his TED Talk on creativity, seeing our body as simply a form of transport for our head. In this disembodied state, it's easy to become trapped by the sweepers of worry and rumination.

When the pandemic shut the world down in 2020, I definitely spent a lot of time in my head. I was obsessed with the news reports and predictions, trying to think through contingency plans and pivots, fearing what might happen. My husband and I were fortunate to be able to work from home, but this also meant spending 24/7 together with our two kids in a small house. Days bled into one another as we juggled work, meals, and online school and worried about people we loved from afar.

I realized I needed a better way to manage my stress, so I signed up for a mindfulness course online. During class, we learned different meditations and how to breathe intentionally in order to regulate our nervous systems. But the easiest tool I learned was a simple question the instructor taught us: *Where are my feet?*

I had to laugh initially because the question seemed so odd, but the instructor was right. Asking it immediately brought me into the present moment. She explained that shifting our attention quickly from an uncomfortable or intense situation to a neutral grounding point (in this case, the soles of our feet) has a calming effect on the body.

This tool, asking yourself where your feet are, can be done anywhere, anytime throughout the day. So can its variations, such as noticing how it feels to sit in your seat, or putting your hands together and feeling the pads of your fingers connect, or doing a body scan to see where there might be tension and then consciously releasing it. All these ways of paying attention to your body can bring you into the here and now.

Center Your Body

Here is a quick way to center your body. First, take a few deep breaths. Then, bring your attention to how you are standing or sitting, where your feet and hands are, and what your posture is like. Envision yourself connecting strongly into the ground, feeling the support of the floor or ground under your feet or the chair you are sitting on. Maintain this awareness for a minute or two.

This is a great tool to use anytime throughout your day, whether you're in a meeting, waiting in traffic, making dinner, or taking a break somewhere.

When you are present in your body, you're better able to recognize what you need, such as taking a break or eating a snack. It's important to take care of yourself with enough sleep, exercise, and healthy food because when you're tired or hungry, you're more likely to become distracted or reactive. You're also more likely to misinterpret the situation around you.

For example, scientists in Israel conducted a study of more than a thousand parole hearings in 2011 and found that judges were more likely to deny parole right before lunch. After lunch, the parole approvals jumped back up to their usual frequency. Hunger and the need for a break evidently skewed the judges' decisions *without their realizing it was happening.* When we feel "off," we may attribute it to something outside ourselves—the environment or another person—when we may just need rest, food, hydration, or a break.

Prioritizing your health, especially when you're going through a challenging transition or juggling many demands on your time, can be difficult. However, that's also when you need it the most, so do what you can. Even small changes such as incorporating more greens into your diet, taking the stairs more often, reducing caffeine and alcohol, and going to sleep a little earlier can add up, making a difference not just in your health but in your ability to be present.

Name Your Emotions to Be Present

There's one more tool to help you be present: noticing and naming your emotions. But before discussing the tool, let's look at why emotions are so important. While scientists debate what exactly emotions are, you likely know from experience that your emotional state can significantly impact you and those around you.

When you are flooded with emotion, it is harder to think clearly or creatively. When you block out emotion, it is harder to empathize and build strong relationships with others.

Emotions play a role in decision-making as well. When you imagine several future possibilities and ask yourself for each one *What would happen if I chose this option? Is this the right direction?* you are assessing that option's pros and cons rationally. But you are also experiencing that outcome emotionally, and how you feel about it informs your decision. Without that emotional input, says neuroscientist Robert Sapolsky, people not only have trouble making decisions; they make bad ones.

Even so, emotions can steer decision-making in unhelpful ways. For example, let's say you're thinking about a potential move to another city. If you are anxious about something having nothing to do with that possible future, that anxiety will taint your thoughts about the move, possibly leading to a poor choice. Even the weather can affect how you're feeling, influencing the decisions you make.

All this to say, our emotions powerfully influence us and how we navigate, so we need to learn how to work with them.

While it may seem counterintuitive, the way to approach emotions is not by ignoring them but by facing them directly. I was reminded of this truth while watching a documentary about buffalo on the Great Plains. As the storm clouds gather and the wind starts whipping, cattle will move away from the storm, trying to outrun it. Buffalo, on the other hand, don't run. They will turn and face the oncoming storm, walking into the snow and wind. They instinctively know that the fastest way past the storm is *through* it.

A simple but effective way to face emotions is to name them (without judgment about whether it's good or bad to have that emotion). Researchers have found that noticing and naming emotions regulates emotional responses so people can *have* an emotion (I *feel* sad) rather than *be* the emotion (I *am* sad). In a study done at UCLA, when participants viewed photos of angry, frustrated, and sad faces, their amygdala (the part of the brain that triggers the fight-flight-freeze reaction) was activated. However, in those participants who were asked to name the emotions they saw in the photos, the amygdala response was dampened, and the part of the prefrontal cortex that helps to process and manage emotions became engaged.

"When you put feelings into words, you're activating this prefrontal region and seeing a reduced response in the amygdala," said Dr. Matthew Lieberman, director of UCLA's Social Cognitive Neuroscience Laboratory and the lead author of the study. "In the same way you hit the brake when you're driving when you see a yellow light, when you put feelings into words, you seem to be hitting the brakes on your emotional responses." Essentially, describing your feelings puts a little distance between you and what you are experiencing, allowing you to feel your emotions without getting lost in them.

While naming emotions is a great tool for moving through them, many people have a limited vocabulary for describing what they are feeling (if they put words to it at all). Saying, "I am happy"—or sad or angry—is a start. However, research shows that using more specific emotional language, what's known as "emotional granularity," is associated with increased resilience and quicker recovery from stress.

What does emotional granularity look like? Instead of the generic "happy," try on a more specific word like elated, amused, appreciative, content, or joyful. Instead of "sad," how about hurt, lonely, melancholic, withdrawn, or skeptical? Instead of "angry," what about furious, agitated, deceived, resentful, or frustrated? Describing more precisely what you're feeling gives you more information about what's happening within you, and that more nuanced understanding helps you make better decisions about what you need or what to do next.

Imagine that a coworker who is writing a report you need for an upcoming deadline tells you at the last minute that it won't be done on time. Instead of thinking, *I'm upset*, slow down for a minute to notice and name in more detail what you're feeling. Maybe you're annoyed. And you're anxious because you now need to scramble to get the report done yourself. You may also be frustrated since the late report puts you in a tough situation with your boss. Deeper down, you may be worried because you've made a few mistakes lately, and not making this deadline would be another one—just as layoffs have started.

As you put into words what you're feeling, you become present to what's truly going on for you. You might then use one of the breathing exercises in this chapter to calm down. This can give you the space to wonder what's happening with your coworker, especially if this behavior is out of character. You might decide to have a conversation with that coworker, your boss, or both—all better options than reacting in frustration or bottling up your worries.

A simple tool to help you notice and name your emotions and, from there, choose your next action is my Notice, Name, Next exercise. It's a reminder to focus on what you're feeling right now and the one thing you need to do next rather than getting caught up in a story of what's happened or what might happen. It's helpful to practice this exercise in low-stress situations so you turn to it automatically during high-stress events.

Notice, Name, Next

- **NOTICE:** Ask yourself, *What's happening for me right now? What am I doing? How am I showing up?*
- **NAME:** Name what you're feeling, being as specific as you can.
- **NEXT:** Ask yourself, *What's needed now?* For example, you might need to take a break, talk with a friend, keep doing what you're doing, or reframe your perspective (we'll look at reframing in chapter four).

Tools for becoming present, such as the ones in this chapter, let us create some space between what happens to us and our response. Even a little bit of distance can help us be more creative and figure out the best next step. Sometimes, that is speeding up to take action; other times, it is slowing down to take a break. Or it may be quickly recovering in the face of fear and pivoting as Wag Dodge did in the Montana wildfire. Even with practice, we will still be reactive at times, but we'll be quicker to notice when we're caught up in the sweepers and to recognize what we need to get back into the flow of the river.

FOR REFLECTION

- What are your "sweepers" (i.e., the worries and distractions that most often snag you and keep you stuck)?

- What is one tool in this chapter that you want to try out (or remember to use) this week?

- When you practice being present, what benefits do you notice for yourself? For others?

3

KNOW WHAT'S CORE FOR YOU

*From Starfish I have learned that
if we keep our core intact, we can
regenerate. We can fall apart,
lose limbs, and . . . grow so many
different arms, depending on what
kind of sea star we are.*

—JOLILLIAN T. ZWERDLING

One of the world's most dangerous stretches of water is at the mouth of the Columbia River, where it empties into the Pacific Ocean in Oregon. The strong currents and giant, shifting sandbar at this intersection of river and ocean make it a treacherous passage for boats. Yet alongside the danger is also beauty. The windswept Oregon coast is stunning, with sandy beaches stretching for miles and numerous sea stacks (large standalone rocks) jutting up just off the shore.

Since we live in the Pacific Northwest, these beaches have been one of my family's favorite road trip destinations. When our kids were little, they loved to explore the tide pools that would form when the tide went out, revealing crabs, sea cucumbers, anemones, and starfish. It was especially fun to see how many of the colorful starfish, or sea stars, we could find among the rugged rocks each visit. But over the years, they became harder and harder to spot. And then they were gone.

In 2013, a disease called sea star wasting syndrome wiped out more than 80 percent of the starfish population along the Pacific Coast from Mexico to Alaska—a devastating hit that scientists struggled to explain. Starfish can regenerate lost arms, but this disease was disintegrating them completely and incredibly fast. One photo series showed a starfish on the first day with a slight mark on one arm, and by the third day, only remnants of the body were left. My family and I started to wonder if we'd ever see starfish in the Pacific Northwest again.

Then scientists began to see one of the species return. It seemed that *Pisaster ochraceus*, the ochre star, had rapidly evolved its genes to adapt to the disease and was starting to increase in number. These starfish were still considered ochre stars, but they were also different.

The return of the ochre star species demonstrates what chemist and Nobel Laureate Ilya Prigogine discovered about how a system— such as an organization, you, me, or the ochre star—responds to significant disruption. When the disruption is moderate, the system can adjust without wholesale transformation—a starfish grows a new arm, or you learn a new skill or behavior. But if the stress and disorder are severe enough, the system will fall apart, releasing its old form. To adapt, it stays in a messy, in-between space for a while before it's able to build back up in a new, more resilient form. In those situations, it's not enough to make small changes. A more fundamental transformation is required: keeping what's core, letting go of what no longer works, and reconfiguring oneself to thrive in the new environment or stage of life.

Prigogine's discovery reminds us that humans, like all systems, evolve into their next iteration not in stable environments but when there is enough disruption and uncertainty to challenge the status quo. In other words, *we need disruption for growth*, and we have an inherent capability to recreate ourselves. While few people wish for challenges, we're more capable of navigating them than we may think, and there are often hidden opportunities amid the losses. However, to prepare ourselves to navigate the changes ahead—both big and small—we need to know what's core for us.

Reflecting on What's Core for You

If I asked you who you are, how would you answer? You might respond with your job title or a role such as mom, dad, sister, or friend; you might describe your personality traits, ethnicity, gender identity, hobbies, values, or beliefs. The ways you could answer are almost countless. More important than your answer, however, is whether you believe you have an answer. The belief that we know who we are provides clarity and comfort, whereas uncertainty about our identity can be incredibly unsettling.

However, people frequently build their identity around an aspect of their life that is not constant, such as a job or a relationship. When that aspect of their life inevitably shifts, they try hard to protect it since losing one's identity feels like losing oneself. They hang on tightly to that definition of who and what they've been, resisting change rather than focusing on who they are becoming.

As the starfish quote that opened the chapter points out, we need something at our core from which we can keep rebuilding our identity in new and different ways. And we each have that within us: our core strengths and core values.

While you likely have many strengths and values, your core strengths and values are the ones that are most important to you, the ones you want to steer by because they keep you on a course that's true to you. Your core values help you sift through choices such as whether or not to take a job or stay in a given situation (relationship, career, community, etc.). Your core strengths are the ones that give you the most energy; you feel the most like yourself when you use them. While your core strengths and core values might evolve over time, they are always with you, no matter what happens to or around you.

CORE STRENGTHS

Sometime in the mid-1940s, a physician by the name of Bernard Haldane moved from England to New York City, hoping to practice medicine. When he learned that his medical credentials wouldn't transfer to the American system and he would have to go back to medical school in the United States, he decided to change careers. He found a job as an editor at the *New York Journal of Commerce*. On the side, he started helping World War II veterans find jobs by identifying what they did well and enjoyed doing that could transfer to the civilian job market. Helping people identify what he later called their "dependable strengths," the strengths they would always have no matter where they went, became his own life's work.

Eventually, Haldane's passion for helping others started to draw attention. Business consultant Peter Drucker described Haldane as a "practical guide, the helping hand, the pathfinder . . . in finding human strength and in making it productive." President John F. Kennedy sent him a telegram that read, "Progress in helping people use their highest skills not only helps the individual worker, it also helps our entire country." Haldane's work, particularly his emphasis on focusing on one's strengths while moving through a transition, significantly influenced the modern-day field of career and employment counseling.

Haldane, along with other pioneers in strengths-based development, reframed how we define ourselves. When we *are* our job, our role, our status, letting go of it is much harder. When our identity is tied to our core strengths, we can be flexible. There is no single way of using our core strengths; we can use them in a variety of tasks and roles, as well as differently across time.

Focusing on our strengths also supports us in accessing our creativity. When we only look for what isn't working—the challenges and our weaknesses as we face those challenges—our brain and body react as if defending against a threat. When we acknowledge the challenges but then look for what *is* working—the opportunities and the strengths we can bring to the situation—we start to see what's possible and are more creative in our ideas and actions. It's like traveling on a river in a kayak or a canoe: If you only focus on the rocks in your way, you're going to run into them. Being aware of those rocks is important, but you need to focus on where the water flows around them in order to move forward.

While knowing our core strengths is important at any point, it's even more important during times of change. Studies have shown that focusing on our strengths leads to higher performance and increased well-being, as well as reduced stress. One of my clients shared that during a big transition in her organization, knowing her core strengths helped her feel more stable and capable. She wrote her strengths down on a Post-it note that she looked at often. It reminded her that she had something of value to bring even when she was outside her comfort zone.

So what is a core strength?

To begin with, strengths are not the same as skills. A skill is something you've learned to do well that you may or may not enjoy doing. For example, during my years working in organizations, I developed the *skill* of organizing detailed information into spreadsheets and other tools to track progress. Other people saw that I did this well and wanted me to do more of it. However, when I think about managing details (and spreadsheets in particular), I want to stick a fork in my eye. That's because managing details is not one of my *strengths*. My core strengths—two of them, anyway—are creating pathways forward and championing and challenging others to reach their full potential. That said, there are many skills connected to my core strengths that I've learned to do well and enjoy, such as coaching, facilitation, and training.

A core strength, then, is something you do well (or have the potential to do well) *and* also enjoy doing. You are most likely using a core strength when you get into what the late psychologist

Mihaly Csikszentmihalyi called "flow." In that state, you are completely immersed in what you are doing; you enjoy the process and the challenges that come with it. It's not necessarily easy, but you are willing to exert the effort because it's inherently rewarding.

You won't utilize your core strengths in everything you do. (I often need to focus on logistics and details, including all the details involved in creating this book.) You may also find yourself relying on your core strengths too much, especially when you're stressed, which can have a negative impact. For example, when trying to navigate a changing situation, someone who excels at planning might keep refining the plan over and over again when they really should start taking action and update the plan as they go. Their strength is planning, but when it's overused, that strength can become a liability.

If you find yourself trapped by your own strengths, use the tools in chapter two, "Be Present," to become more aware of what you're feeling and doing. Then, from this broader perspective, determine the best approach going forward, which might be doing something that isn't a strength but is better suited for the situation.

Everyone has core strengths. It can take time and some trial and error to recognize what yours are. They may also be qualities so natural to you that you don't realize they are core strengths. However, the effort to explore and identify your core strengths will pay off, since once you know what they are, you can lean on them intentionally (and know which things aren't your strengths so you know when to lean on other people for help). When you do that, you're likely to find your efforts supercharged, as if you've caught a helpful current in a river.

Identify Your Core Strengths

Many assessments, processes, and tools have been developed to help people identify their core strengths. The following is a simple, effective approach you can do on your own:

1. **Reflect:** Reflect on situations in your personal and professional life where you felt energized and you were able to bring value in some way. What specifically were you doing? How were you showing up? Jot these down. Examples include building strong partnerships, doing detailed planning, creating artwork, or being empathetic.

2. **Ask:** Ask five or more people in different areas of your life what they see as your greatest strengths. What do you do especially well? What do they appreciate about your approach? If you prefer not to ask others, instead reflect on compliments you have received. Write these down.

3. **Review and Name:** Review your reflections and the input from others, looking for patterns or themes that could be strengths. Identify three strengths that you want to keep using in the future. Give each one a name you find memorable and meaningful. Alternatively, name each one according to the role you play while using it, such as connector, pathfinder, relationship builder, disrupter, calming influencer, or storyteller.

CORE VALUES

In my work with both individuals and organizations, I have repeatedly seen the benefit of knowing one's core values. Core values are the principles or beliefs that guide actions and decisions. While they may evolve over time, core values are generally stable and can serve as an important navigational tool when everything else about a situation is murky, which is often the case during a transition. But thinking about your values once and putting them aside won't be very useful. You need to know what your core values are *and* keep reminding yourself of them so they can guide you forward.

John Kroger, a former attorney general and U.S. Navy chief learning officer, now runs a leadership institute for public leaders. When I asked him how he navigates uncertainty, knowing and reflecting on his core values was at the top of his list. For more than thirty years, he's kept a simple yet effective practice.

"No matter where I am, I always have a whiteboard on the wall where I list the core values I'm trying to bring to a particular job and the strategic goals that I'm trying to achieve," he explained. "I look at it ten or fifteen times a day to reorient myself, especially when it's chaotic or there's a crisis. I'm really visual, so it's grounding to have the physical words in my workspace reminding me what I need to do and how I want to interact with other people." He went on to say that in really volatile situations where you find yourself stepping back to rethink your direction and your goals, it's your values that help guide your decisions.

There is power not only in knowing your core values but also in taking time to reflect on them. One proven way to reflect on your values is to write about them. Study after study has shown the benefits of not only picking a top value but also writing about why it's important. A meta-analysis of these studies showed the numerous payoffs from this additional step, including students achieving higher grades, diabetics and smokers finding increased motivation to change their habits, and people in conflict being more willing to work towards shared solutions. Other studies show how referencing one's values yields more creative problem-solving, which is a superpower in times of uncertainty.

Another way to reflect on your core values is to assess if you are making decisions and acting in alignment with them. A simple way to do this is to write down your values and then, for each one, ask yourself, *How am I demonstrating this value in my life right now?* If you find there is a gap between what you value and what you're doing, ask yourself, *What do I need to do to be in alignment?*

In certain situations or times of your life, one core value may become more prominent for you; for example, family has become more important to me as I've gotten older. Or two or more of your values may be in conflict, a common example among professionals being the struggle between valuing family and valuing career. In such moments, you may have to get creative about how to move forward, finding a way to honor both, or at least being conscious of the trade-offs you are making.

Identify Your Core Values

The following reflection questions are designed to surface clues about what's most important to you, what you value most:

- Identify several important decisions you have made in the last five years. Then, ask yourself, *What values do I believe influenced those decisions?* Some examples are honesty, family, flexibility, justice, relationships, courage, learning, and achievement.

- Identify three people you admire. Then, ask yourself, *What values do these people demonstrate that I feel are important?*

- Ask yourself, *What am I the most grateful for? What am I the proudest of in my life?*

As you consider your answers to these questions, pay attention to which values show up repeatedly. What are the top three values that seem most important to you?

Knowing what's core for you is key for effectively adapting to change. Former Starbucks head of human resources Lucy Helm underscored this during a recent conversation: "When you have that core, then you can build from that whenever something changes," she said. "I've coached a lot of people through change, and it's important to know what motivates you, what matters to you. Otherwise, you're in quicksand; there's nothing stable."

When we know and remember what's core for us, the brain receives the signal that, regardless of what is going on around us and within us, something at our core is stable. With that inner stability in place, we are able to turn our attention outward to find ways to put our core strengths and values into action.

Putting What's Core into Action

Konstantinos, also known as Kosta, had worked for twenty-five years as a marketing and communications specialist when the global financial crisis of 2008 made its way to Greece. As the country reeled in economic instability and a historic recession, Kosta, like thousands of others, lost his job. After two years of not finding work, at forty-seven years old, he was forced to move in with his mother. It was a challenging time as he and his mom struggled to stay afloat on her monthly pension, which covered rent and little else.

One day, when Kosta was walking through a market in Athens, he came across two children fighting over rotten fruit in a garbage can. It was hard to watch, but even harder was witnessing people just walking by. Reflecting on that moment later, he said, "What bothered me most was the lack of concern shown by passersby—in other words, the indifference. That showed me there is something missing in society, and I decided to do something about it."

Kosta began the next day. He made cheese sandwiches and handed them to people who were searching in the trash for food. When they refused his offer, he thought perhaps they felt ashamed or didn't trust him, so he sat down to eat beside them, starting a conversation. This act shifted the situation from a charitable transaction to the very human interaction of eating a meal together.

As he continued providing food for people in the streets, Kosta decided he wanted to not only feed anyone who was hungry but also build relationships through conversation. He eventually started the organization O Allos Anthropos, Greek for "the other human," and began cooking food seven days a week, providing opportunities for people to eat together while talking with and learning from one another.

I not only find Kosta's story inspiring because of what he's done for his community, but I also see it as a great example of applying one's core strengths and values in new ways. Kosta couldn't have known in advance the new direction his life would take, but by focusing on what was needed around him, he found a way forward. It's where our core strengths, core values, and what's needed around us intersect that we often figure out what's next. This intersection is our purpose.

Purpose is sometimes viewed as a fixed thing, as in "find your life purpose," which suggests that a single purpose for your life is waiting for you out there somewhere, and your task is to go find it. I don't see it that way. While some people may have a single purpose that remains a constant over time, that's not the case for everyone. More often, what remains constant are people's core strengths and values, which can be applied differently as what's needed around them shifts over time and across circumstances. This more adaptive, creative approach to purpose was summed up well by astrophysicist Carl Sagan: "We *make* our purpose."

Even though purpose focuses our attention outside ourselves, we also benefit. Research has shown that having a purpose, which gives our lives a sense of meaning, correlates with increased resilience, improved health, better work performance, and even a longer life. Having a purpose is especially beneficial during uncertain or challenging times. According to research conducted by McKinsey & Company during the coronavirus pandemic, people who felt they had a purpose reported *five times* greater well-being than those who didn't.

However, sometimes the purpose behind what you're doing is hidden, and you need to broaden your perspective to find it, as the following parable shows:

> Three stonecutters were hard at work on the same
> project. When asked what they were doing, the
> first one responded, "I'm cutting stone." The sec-
> ond one said, "I'm working on a wall." The third
> one exclaimed, "I'm building a cathedral!"

The differences in their answers are a matter of perspective.
The third stonecutter saw each stone he cut and each wall he built
as part of a bigger, meaningful project—so big that he might not
see its end, since the cathedral likely wouldn't be completed in
his lifetime.

The wisdom of this story is paralleled by modern-day research.
More than twenty years ago, management scholars Amy Wrzesniewski and Jane Dutton introduced the concept of "job
crafting." People who are job crafters intentionally and proactively
shape their jobs over time. They adjust what they do to align with
their strengths and revise what they see as the purpose of their
work to make it more meaningful. Compared with other work-
ers, they are generally better performers and more satisfied in both
work and life.

In a study Wrzesniewski and Dutton did with twenty-eight
hospital cleaners, those who were job crafters viewed themselves
as contributing to patients' healing. One cleaner who worked in
a long-term rehabilitation ward, where many patients were in a
coma, regularly rearranged the art on the walls. This wasn't part of
her job, she told a researcher, but she hoped that shifting the environment would in some way support the patients' recovery. While
her job description wasn't different than that of other cleaners, she

had a purpose. Her work was more meaningful to her because she knew *why* she did it.

How Purpose Can Guide You

From an early age, my client Lauren knew exactly what she wanted to be when she grew up: a journalist. She would spend hours writing, filling journal after journal while considering how to make her dream a reality. After college, she held a series of jobs in publishing, honing her strengths in writing and story development—but she had entered the field during the disruptive shift to digital, and journalism jobs were disappearing. She faced a choice point: Would she keep trying to get a job in an increasingly tough market or let go of being a journalist and pursue her dream in a different way? She chose the latter. To find her new direction, she asked herself, *What do I love about journalism?*

For Lauren, journalism was about storytelling. She especially loved story as a vehicle for change. She also realized that working with story isn't solely the domain of writers and journalists; there are many ways to be what she called a "changemaking storyteller."

Getting clear on this as her purpose—where her strengths and values came together in service of others—opened Lauren to opportunities she would not have considered as a journalist. Over the years, her career journey has spanned several industries and roles. She's now a marketing executive at a commercial real estate company that originally hired her to help reposition the company for a changing market. She believed that a simple shift in narrative could change the trajectory of an organization, and that's just what happened. The organization's purpose wasn't just about selling real estate but creating a compelling environment for their customers, the tenants, and ultimately building a positive and impactful future of work. When that purpose became clear, it guided their next iteration as a company.

"Throughout my career, I've stepped into roles I wasn't sure I could do," Lauren said. "But I was able to tackle that uncertainty by leaning into what I do know—I have the ability to help others tell their story and articulate why it matters . . . this is what gets me excited to get out of bed in the morning."

When you reflect on your core strengths and values and how to apply them to what's needed around you right now, it can reveal a purpose going forward, as we saw with Kosta and Lauren. Once you have a purpose, it can be a resource as you move through change, as it was for Lauren, helping you see opportunities you might not otherwise see.

To explore what your purpose is right now, check out the Create a Purpose Statement tool. Crafting a concise statement of purpose and posting it somewhere you'll see it regularly helps you keep in mind the difference you want to make. It can also reframe the more mundane parts of your life and work into a meaningful bigger picture, shifting your perspective from "cutting stone" to "building a cathedral."

Create a Purpose Statement

To clarify and articulate your purpose, create a short purpose statement. Here's how to do it:

- First, refer back to your core strengths and values (see the Identify Your Core Strengths and Identify Your Core Values tools in this chapter).

- Then, think about what's needed around you or in the world today, and reflect on the following question: *What's needed right now that I want to help with given my strengths, values, and experiences?*

- Finally, create a brief statement or phrase that captures the essence of what's most meaningful for you.

- Try out the statement for a few weeks before going back to update or refine it.

Don't worry about creating the perfect purpose statement. Sometimes, people get stuck in endless wordsmithing as they try to come up with the perfect phrase. Just write whatever feels meaningful for you right now. You can always revise it, especially as you learn more about what's important to you and what's needed around you.

A purpose statement can be quite general ("to spark joy"), more specific ("to advocate for equitable health systems"), or something in between, like mine: "to help people create what's next." It's a high-level headline, not a list of your strengths, values, and all the things you do. Its function is to remind you of *why* you do what you do. During a transition, it can guide you toward a new future.

"Developing a purpose statement has been invaluable to me," a client wrote in an email after I helped her draft a purpose statement. After losing her job, she had taken a temporary position to pay the bills, giving her some space to figure out what was next. "It not only gave me clarity for my future but affirmed where I am now. It holds space for me in between the 'now' and 'not yet.'"

It holds space for me in between the "now" and "not yet."

I loved this reflection. When I asked her to say more about it during a follow-up call, she explained, "I tend to stay focused on what I haven't figured out yet or done yet, and then I miss things in the present. Although my current role isn't right for me, I can see now which parts of it are aligned with my purpose, as well as the gaps." Having her purpose articulated in a purpose statement allowed her to make the most of where she was right then, even as it guided her choices about what (and what not) to pursue next.

Angela Duckworth, author of the book *Grit*, talks about the importance of having a "compass," her term for what I call a purpose statement. Her own compass is to "use psychological science to help kids thrive." Crafting that statement took years of exploration as she changed careers, failed, let go of projects, and pursued unexpected paths, she writes, but once she had it, it became an invaluable and consistent guide.

Knowing what's core for you is essential in changing times. When you know and remember your core strengths and values, you can adapt or reinvent yourself again and again. You can create a purpose that will guide you forward. And you can travel with an internal feeling of stability, even as everything else keeps shifting.

FOR REFLECTION

- What are two of your core strengths? What do you enjoy about using them?

- What are two of your core values? Why are they important to you?

- How do you currently put what's core for you into action—in service of something bigger than you?

4

REFRAME YOUR PERSPECTIVE

As my context changes,
so does what I believe.

—AMY TAN

The Yangtze River, the third longest river in the world, begins on the Tibetan Plateau in Western China and flows eastward across the country before reaching the East China Sea. As it winds its way through various ecosystems, it creates an agricultural division. For thousands of years, people to the south of the Yangtze have typically grown rice while people to the north have focused on wheat farming. Here's what's interesting: It turns out that growing up and living on one side of the river or the other shapes people's outlooks differently, even today.

In a study published in 2014, researchers conducted a series of tests with more than a thousand students in different regions along the Yangtze River. They found that students who lived south of the river showed more collaborative, holistic thinking compared with students north of the river, who demonstrated more self-reliant, individualistic thinking. The researchers believe this is because the cultural mindsets associated with rice farming and with wheat farming have seeped into the local culture for generations. Rice growing is labor intensive, and the traditional system of irrigating rice fields requires collaboration among farms. Wheat farming takes less labor and relies on rainfall, so farmers work more independently. These age-old farming practices seem to have influenced the students' responses on the tests, even when they had no direct connection to farming themselves.

When I came across this study, I was fascinated. It's such a clear illustration of how culture and environment can "frame" our view of the world—and therefore how different people can interpret the same situation in very different ways. That's because every person carries their own mental frames, or what psychologists call *schemas*, which have formed over time according to factors such as the person's memories of past experiences, the culture where they live, who they spend time with, how they were raised, and the generation they were born into.

Our mental frames determine what we see and how we interpret it. The fact that they usually do this without our awareness explains why it's so easy to stay in habitual thought patterns and behaviors. However, by using perspective-shifting tools, we can notice and revise our mental frames—we can *reframe* what we see. With the reframing, we can better perceive alternative, often more creative ways to respond to whatever change we are navigating.

Don't Get Stuck in Your Mental Frames

Every second, the human brain processes some eleven million pieces of information. We're aware of only about forty bits of that information, which leaves a *lot* of information being processed outside our conscious awareness. Some of this data concerns basic body functions that are rarely noticed unless there's a problem: food digesting, saliva swallowing, and eyes blinking, for instance. If we were aware of everything going on both within and outside us, we would be overwhelmed and unable to function, so the brain keeps out of our consciousness whatever we don't need to be aware of in the moment. This is why a person who has learned to ride a bike doesn't have to think about how to do it anymore; they just pedal and go.

Similarly, our brain uses mental frames to make sense of incoming data about the world around us *without our realizing it*. The students in the Yangtze River study likely had no idea that the traditional farming practices where they lived had shaped their mental framing, which influenced their test responses. Our mental frames are typically invisible to us, much like water is to fish, as writer David Foster Wallace described during a speech:

> There are these two young fish swimming along, and they happen to meet an older fish swimming the other way, who nods at them and says, "Morning, boys, how's the water?" And the two young fish swim on for a bit, and then eventually one of them looks over at the other and goes, "What the hell is water?"

Your mental frames inform your decisions and behaviors every day, sometimes in unhelpful or even harmful ways—stereotyping and negative bias being two examples. As you pay attention to how you're seeing yourself, other people, or a situation, you can begin to notice your frames at work. This creates an opportunity for you to reframe your perspective when it's not serving you and others. As you practice reframing over time, you expand your perspective and are less likely to get stuck in a single point of view.

Our mental frames are particularly influential when we're navigating the unknown. Because we instinctively dislike uncertainty, we tend to default unconsciously to the comforting familiarity of our mental frames. Instead of thinking broadly to find a creative way forward, our perspective narrows as we try to come up with an answer—any answer—that moves us out of the murkiness of ambiguity. We often slip into either/or thinking, convinced that the polarized options we see in this limited state are the only ones available:

> *I can either quit my job or stay put and be miserable.*
>
> *You're either on board with this or you're not.*
>
> *If I'm right, then you're wrong.*
>
> *I can keep pouring money into this idea or cut my losses now.*
>
> *I've tried that before; it won't work.*

Whether we realize it or not, we're seeking safety in the form of quick and certain answers.

The human need for certainty is strong and can drive behavior in perplexing ways. In one study, participants preferred to know *for certain* they would receive an electric shock than to know their chance of receiving a shock was 50/50. Not knowing was worse than actually getting shocked!

However, here's the thing: Uncertainty *helps* us be creative. That's because uncertainty pulls us off autopilot, requiring us to pay attention. When the predictability of certainty is removed, we are forced to look for new routes that take us in directions we hadn't considered before.

Thinking about uncertainty in this way can itself be a reframing; you may not have considered uncertainty in this light before. And that's the point: to be able to view what's in front of us in new, original ways.

Reframe with Metaphors

One effective tool for reframing your perspective is metaphor. A metaphor is a figure of speech in which one object or idea is described in terms of another: "She's an open book," for example. But metaphors are more than colorful statements that can spice up a conversation; they also influence our reasoning, emotions, and actions. We often use them without realizing it, which is why they are powerful for reframing. Once we notice a metaphor we're using, we can intentionally use a different one, which changes what we see.*

---

* While metaphors can be powerful tools for reframing, they can be confusing and not as useful for some people if their brain processes metaphors literally.

The influence of metaphors has been the subject of several studies. One study published in 2011 showed that the metaphor you use to describe a problem can influence how you envision its solution. The researchers asked two groups of participants to come up with solutions to the high crime level in a city. In the course of presenting the crime information, they spoke of crime as if it were a virus infecting the city to one group and as if it were a wild beast preying on the city to the other. The participants in the "virus" group came up with solutions related to root causes of crime and preventive measures such as education. The ideas offered by participants in the "wild beast" group centered on capturing and jailing criminals and creating harsher laws. The metaphors had clearly shaped the participants' thinking. However, when the participants were asked what had influenced their ideas, no one mentioned the metaphors. They were part of the water, and no one saw them.

The effect of metaphors on goal setting has been studied as well. Szu-chi Huang and Jennifer Aaker at Stanford University's business school have found that which metaphor people use when viewing a goal can determine whether, after reaching the goal, they continue the actions that helped them achieve it. "Many times in our research we observed that after people accomplished [their] goals, they didn't have something to strive for anymore, and we immediately saw a drop in motivation," Dr. Huang shared with me. "In some cases, it's okay to engage with a goal and then disengage from it when it's done. . . . But we found in other situations, like learning and health, that viewing goals like a destination is actually harmful, because if we stop the behaviors that helped us achieve the goal, we end up losing the progress we've made."

Huang and Aaker wondered what would happen if people stopped framing their goal as a destination and instead focused on the journey to reach that goal. Would changing the metaphor change people's long-term behavior?

To find out, they conducted six studies—five in the United States and one in Ghana—with more than sixteen hundred people who had achieved a range of goals, including losing weight and completing an education program. In each study, they presented some participants with journey-metaphor framing, some with destination-metaphor framing, and some with no metaphor at all. For example, in Ghana, they set up exit interviews for graduates of a Stanford executive education program. Some interviews were scripted to encourage the interviewees to describe their achievement in terms of the journey metaphor, others in terms of the destination metaphor. (Those not interviewed served as a control group.) Six months later, the graduates who had used the journey metaphor were the most likely to still be applying what they had learned. The results were so striking that journey framing was subsequently used in Stanford's Ghana program for all students.

When the research team dug into why referencing a journey was so influential, they found that it encouraged participants to focus on how they had grown personally in the process. Dr. Huang told me, "When we included the journey framing, it made people reflect not just on what they had achieved but on all the effort and struggles it took to get from where they had been to where they are today. . . . It wasn't just the actions of eating healthy, or being diligent about studying, or putting in the extra effort at work to reach a goal; it was also about their identity. And if these actions are aligned with who you are now, you're going to continue those behaviors into the future."

Huang and Aaker later expanded their research to look at whether the journey metaphor could be helpful to people going through significant change. "We have early-stage data showing connections between using a journey metaphor and building resilience," Dr. Huang told me in 2021. "We think this is because journeys have lots of ups and downs, and so [the journey metaphor] reminds us that when we are in a down point, it's not forever. It will go back up eventually, so people are less likely to give up."

Her comment reinforces the value of the journey mapping tool in chapter one ("Expect a Journey"). Mapping your journey— reflecting on how you navigated past twists and turns and who you became in the process—helps you remember going forward that a setback is not forever; it's only a point in the journey.

Dr. Huang stressed that, to be effective, the journey metaphor needs to be used with intention: "You hear 'journey' used a lot, but our default is to focus more on the destination. We need to remind ourselves to *think* about the journey, to really sit down and reflect on it, since there are so many benefits to doing that. . . . It's something we need to practice."

Choose Your Metaphor Wisely

Metaphors help us grapple with ideas like the future and uncertainty, which are abstract concepts, by tying them to physical experiences. For example, after reading this book, you're more likely to associate moving through change with navigating the shifting channels of a river. What you may not realize is that as you make that association, your brain actually *maps* it.

Dr. Krish Sathian, a neurologist and cognitive neuroscientist at Penn State, has used functional magnetic resonance imaging (fMRI) to identify the areas of the brain that activate as various metaphors are used. He and his colleagues found, for example, that when study participants thought about the statement "I am having a rough day," the same sensory regions of the brain lit up as when the participants touched something rough.

We don't just think and talk with metaphors; the brain responds as if we are physically experiencing them. This may be why metaphors have such a powerful effect on our thoughts and actions. I've seen this firsthand in coaching sessions: clients coming up with new ideas and possible paths forward by using a metaphor to reframe what they're doing. One client and I identified LEGOs (the plastic interlocking block toys) as a metaphor to help her generate new product marketing ideas; another used a skiing metaphor to feel more confident going through a tricky transition. With many clients, I've referenced being "30,000 feet up" or "standing on a balcony" to get a big-picture perspective.

Reframe with Metaphors

When you are feeling stuck or are facing a new or unknown context, brainstorm metaphors that could help you creatively contemplate next steps. For example: This situation is a _____ (puzzle, dance, board

continued

game, point on the journey, science project, archaeology site, marathon, etc.). Write them down as they come to mind. Then, choose one you'd like to explore.

Think about the parallels between the metaphor you chose and the situation you are facing. If it's a "science project," what experiments can you do? If it's a "marathon," what might you need to sustain your energy for the long distance?

Play with the different metaphors, noticing what possibilities and new perspectives each one opens up for you.

However, as Huang and Aaker discovered with the destination metaphor, certain metaphors don't always serve us well. When a client shared with me her concerns about her new leadership role at work, she said, "I just don't want to be a bull in a china shop." The comment seemed harmless, but as we moved on to brainstorming her next steps, I noticed a cautiousness about her. At that point, I paused our conversation and repeated back to her what she had said. She replied, "I didn't even realize I'd said that."

We often don't notice the metaphors we use, but once we become aware of what we're saying, we have a choice. This awareness is important because the metaphors we use can shape our behaviors. Once my client knew what she had said (and may have said, or thought, many times before), she could decide whether that metaphor helped her think creatively as she moved forward or if a different framing would be better.

Consider how other common metaphors might shape your expectations and behaviors. Trying to "get on track" with your career implies that your career is a single, straight path, and if you venture off it, something is wrong. "Battling" cancer suggests that patients "lose" when they don't go into remission. When an argument is framed as a "war," the people involved are likely to pick sides, with someone winning and someone losing—which is counterproductive if they are trying to move forward together.

When you notice that you're using a certain metaphor, ask yourself, *Is this metaphor helping me be creative?* If your answer is no, then ask, *What different metaphor can I use?* Changing metaphors can change not only your perception of your current context but also what you think is possible. As the authors of *Metaphors We Live By* put it, "New metaphors have the power to create a new reality."

Reframe by Shifting Your Focus

Besides working with metaphor, another way to reframe your perspective is to shift your focus. Your perception of the world around you isn't a photograph of an objective reality; it's more like a painting of which you're the artist. Your mental frames shape that reality, and that "reality" can change as you shift your focus to see it from a different vantage point, prompting a reframe. The following are some of my favorite focus-shifting tools:

Zoom in and out. Our perspective on something shifts as we look at it in more detail (zoom in) or in a bigger context (zoom out). When my dad was navigating the Tanana River, his perspective would zoom in on detail when he focused on the changing channels right in front of the boat or checked that everyone in the boat was doing okay. It would zoom out when he was paying attention to the overall patterns in the river or scanning the horizon for weather changes. We need both perspectives, but sometimes, we can get stuck in one or the other.

To zoom in, ask, *What do I need to look at more closely right now? What important details, nuances, or subtle shifts might I be missing?*

To zoom out, ask, *What's the broader context here? Who or what can help me see the bigger picture—the purpose, trends, and patterns?*

Flip the framing. Because of the negativity bias that comes with being human, we tend to focus on problems that need to be fixed rather than looking for what's already working and building on that. While problems should not be ignored, creative paths forward are often found by reframing the question "What's not working?" as "Where is it working, and why?"

A great example is Jerry and Monique Sternin's work in the early 1990s addressing child malnutrition in Vietnamese villages. Save the Children, an NGO, was approached by the Vietnamese government for assistance, but when the Sternins, who worked for Save the Children, arrived in the country, they were told they had only six months to produce results. The impossibility of this deadline forced them to look at the situation in a new way: flipping the framing from focusing on the problem to searching for bright spots. They partnered with local staff to identify and interview mothers whose children were not malnourished: *What were they doing differently?*

They learned that these moms had introduced a few small changes in their children's diet. They included sweet potato greens and tiny shrimp and crabs (readily available and nutritious but not usually given to children) along with the usual rice. They also fed their children several small meals throughout the day—easier for children to digest—rather than a large meal once a day. By improvising with what was available, these women had changed the trajectory of their children's health.

In small village cooking groups, these moms shared with others what had worked for them. Within a two-year period, child malnourishment in Vietnam's villages was reduced by 65–85 percent.

Another way to flip the framing in your own life is with a gratitude practice. Spend a few minutes once a day thinking about what you're grateful for, shifting your focus away from what's not working, what you don't have, or what you haven't accomplished yet. Identify three things you are thankful for in that moment. They can be big or small—the problem at work you recently solved or the cup of coffee you are sipping on right now. You can write them in a journal or simply say them to yourself. Research shows that when people regularly reflect on their lives from a perspective of gratitude, their health and well-being improve, and they have more mental resilience in challenging times.

Consider what's missing. When Allied fighter planes were being shot down in large numbers during World War II, the U.S. military sought ways to reduce the number of losses. They looked at returning planes and considered putting metal armor—so heavy that it could not be used all over the plane—on the areas with the most damage. However, mathematician Abraham Wald reasoned counterintuitively that the armor should be put where there was little or no damage since that's likely where the downed planes, the ones that didn't return, were hit. The damage on the planes that made it back showed where they could be damaged and still fly—which was not where the armor was needed.

While the accuracy of this story is not confirmed, it's still a good reminder that what's visible or present right now may not be the whole story. Applying this in a business setting, if a business owner sends out a survey to current customers only, the input of customers who quit the business's services will be missed. Yet the feedback of these past clients on what to improve could be uniquely valuable.

The following are questions you can ask yourself (and others) to help surface what's hidden:

- *What's not being said that needs to be?*
- *What don't I/we know about this situation?*
- *What or whose perspective is missing?*

Reframe stress. When we stretch ourselves or try things for the first time, we may feel stressed and anxious. What determines whether we'll be negatively affected by that stress is not how much of it we're experiencing but *how we view it*. For example, research has shown that test takers and public speakers perform better when they reframe the stress-induced nervous energy they feel beforehand as their body simply preparing them to tackle a challenge.

Another way of reframing stress is to remember that we get stressed about things that matter to us. So rather than focusing on being stressed, shift your attention to the meaning behind it. Ask yourself, *Why does this matter to me?* The answer might be that you want to support your team or change a harmful system. It could be that you want to provide for your family, learn something new, or be of service to others. You can't get rid of stress, but by reframing it, you can change how it impacts you.

Do a 10-10-10 reflection. The 10-10-10 reflection, a form of zooming out in time, is especially useful when making an important decision. Created by business writer Suzy Welch, it focuses your attention on the consequences of a decision in three different time frames. It's a quick way to "try on" the decision and play it out down the road, exploring what you might gain or lose over time.

Think of an important decision you need to make. Then, ask yourself, *What are the consequences of my decision*

- *ten minutes from now?*
- *ten months from now?*
- *ten years from now?*

This exercise is not an attempt to predict the future. Its purpose is to surface what's most important to you. As an example, the decision to start my own business was not easy to make. The initial consequences—the ten-minute perspective—meant having some hard conversations with my husband and my boss. At ten months, there would likely be a dip in my income and a loss of identity as I switched from a traditional job with a nice title to making up my role as I went. But at ten years, I would be a different person, likely grateful to my former self for taking the risk. The value ten-plus years out was reinforced by my dad, who said, "If you don't do it, you'll get to my age and wonder *what if*. . .?" While the ten-year view didn't make me any less scared, it helped me reach clarity on what I needed to do.

Reframe through Other People's Perspectives

While we can reframe our perspective on our own using the tools in this chapter, one of the most powerful ways to reframe is to see the situation through other people's eyes. And the more diverse perspectives we're exposed to, the better.

Our instinctive response in the face of uncertainty or change is to connect with people *who are like us*. This is a throwback to when survival depended on being with our tribe. As much as familiarity offers comfort, it also gets in the way of creativity. When everyone around us thinks like we do, we are less likely to stretch our own thinking.

One memorable experience of reframing through a perspective very different from mine happened to me in 2001. I was in my late twenties and in a major transition. I had left my corporate job in Chicago, moved to Seattle, and was trying to figure out what was next in my career and life. I was in what I would later call the Regroup part of the Change Curve, and I hated it. I didn't want to be suspended in that "in-between" place; I wanted *the answer*.

Travel has always served as a balm of sorts when I'm in

transition—it helps me get out of my own head and see the world from a new perspective. When my then-roommate asked if I wanted to go with her on a trekking trip to Nepal, I quickly said yes.

Even while we were hiking through stunning Himalayan landscapes, my impatience with not knowing what was next for me back home persisted—until one evening at dinner with a Nepali family. The father said something that has stuck with me ever since. Many people travel to Nepal searching for something, he said, "always searching." I felt a little embarrassed, realizing he had just described me. I was one of those searchers. His words brought about a fundamental reframe: Why was I searching for some magical answer? While I was searching, he was living.

You don't need to travel halfway around the world to experience a reframe by looking through someone else's eyes. Stay curious and open to the people around you, especially those whose lived experiences and mental frames differ from yours. More creative outcomes are possible when you suspend that knee-jerk reaction to rely on your own viewpoint and experience.

This is what the pharmaceutical company Eli Lilly discovered. Around the time I was trekking in Nepal, Alph Bingham, Eli Lilly's vice president of research and development, was trying to convince a top executive that the company should crowdsource solutions to some problems that had their internal scientists stumped. Bingham believed that creative ideas would surface when outside knowledge was invited into the process. There was fear and resistance among some senior leaders about publicly sharing this information, as well as a disbelief that anyone besides Lilly's top scientists could come up with solutions. However, Bingham got the green light and posted the problems on a website to see what would happen.

Novel ideas started to pour in. A lawyer came up with a solution to a molecular synthesis problem. While not a scientist, he knew enough about the topic from his work on chemical patents to understand the issue while having enough distance from it to think outside the box. In the words of Karim Lakhani, codirector of the Laboratory for Innovation Science at Harvard, "Big innovation most often happens when an outsider who may be far away from the surface of the problem reframes the problem in a way that unlocks the solution."

When I'm training members of a team to work effectively and creatively together, I stress to them the importance of seeking out other people, both within and outside the team, who will see a problem or situation from a different perspective. However, when we connect and work with people who are different from us, whether in communication style, professional experience, race, gender identity, generation, or any number of differences, there's the potential for friction because of our varied experiences and viewpoints. While that friction can be uncomfortable, it can also spark creative ideas and solutions that no one person could come up with on their own.

Reframe through Other People's Perspectives

When you are struggling with a problem or stuck in a particular perspective, reach out to people who are likely to view your situation in a different way. The following reflection questions can help you decide who to approach:

- Who has a different approach to solving problems? For example, if you're methodical and logical, who is more spontaneous and imaginative?

- Whose professional or lived experience is completely different from yours?

- If you are more pessimistic, who can help you see the optimistic side of things? Alternatively, if you're more optimistic, who can help you see the potential barriers and challenges you may be ignoring?

- Who do you regularly disagree with or find annoying? What can you learn from them?

Reframing your perspective is a powerful practice. It keeps your mind open, nimble, and adaptive. But noticing and revising your mental frames takes intention and mental energy, which are less available when your nervous system is in a fight-flight-freeze response. If you find yourself flooded with emotion or otherwise in a reactive state, take a few minutes to calm your body and become present using the tools in chapter two ("Be Present") before using the reframing tools in this chapter. Another way to regulate your nervous system before reframing is to connect with supportive people, which is the topic of the next chapter.

FOR REFLECTION

- How do you view uncertainty? Do you tend to see it as a problem to be dealt with or as an opportunity for creativity?

- Consider a goal you have right now. Notice whether you are focusing on the goal as a destination or focusing on the journey to get to the goal.

- When has someone helped you see a situation, problem, or opportunity from a different perspective?

5

CONNECT WITH OTHERS

Whether you are overwhelmed by your own stress or the suffering of others, the way to find hope is to connect.

—KELLY MCGONIGAL

Joseph Campbell spent much of his career thinking about journeys. As a scholar of comparative mythology, he noticed a common pattern among many myths and religions from around the world that he labeled the Hero's Journey. In his 1949 book, *The Hero with a Thousand Faces*, Campbell describes this timeless trek. It begins when the hero responds to the "call to adventure" and sets out on a journey past the edge of what's known into the unknown—the sea, the jungle, the dark woods, the belly of the whale. The hero wrestles with various challenges and takes on difficult tasks before returning home to share the lessons learned and gifts gained with others, knowing that another journey will begin sometime in the future.

This storyline very likely sounds familiar. It's one of the most common narrative arcs used by authors and filmmakers, including George Lucas, who said that Campbell's work had a big influence on the Star Wars films. The Hero's Journey describes the process of personal transformation and growth, which begins when "the familiar life horizon has been outgrown; the old concepts, ideals, and emotional patterns no longer fit; the time for the passing of a threshold is at hand." This archetypal narrative has reminded humans across ages and continents to expect a journey and be prepared for the transitions that inevitably come with it.

What tend to get highlighted in these narratives are the individual heroes and heroines, their struggles, and their bravery. What is often overlooked is how much help they receive along the way. As Campbell describes in *The Hero with a Thousand Faces*, there are always allies—companions and guides—who show up at key points on the journey to offer support. In myths and stories, they appear as the sage who provides direction or the stranger who offers a gift that later saves the hero's or heroine's life. In our day-to-day lives, they are the friend who listens when we're at our lowest or the colleague who provides advice right when we need it.

The truth is this: None of us gets anywhere on our own. We may think we can go it alone, but we need other people. The value of connecting with others is not simply in the help or advice we receive but also in the *feeling of being connected*. When we feel the support of others, we're more likely to explore, stretch ourselves, and find a way forward through the harder times.

I learned about Joseph Campbell and the Hero's Journey from my high school English teacher. Mrs. Horikawa was one of my all-time favorite teachers, not just because she made learning fun but also because she was an important sounding board for me as I thought about my future. She always had great questions and perspectives and was incredibly supportive. After I left Alaska for college, I would try to meet up with her whenever I returned home. During one visit, she gave me the VHS tapes of the 1988 PBS documentary that featured journalist Bill Moyers interviewing Joseph Campbell. I tried to watch them at the time, but they didn't grab my attention; I was too busy with school and life. Then, a few years after graduating from college, I rediscovered those tapes.

I was living in Chicago and focused on my plan for becoming an adult: Get a good job, find an apartment, establish a routine, and try to feel like I know what I'm doing. While I appeared outwardly to have a lot going for me, inwardly, I was miserable. I realized my corporate career wasn't the right fit; I was in a dead-end, toxic relationship; and numerous health issues made me a frequent visitor at the doctor's office. My life seemed to be falling apart just as it was getting started.

I began obsessing and worrying about death, reading *The Tibetan Book of Living and Dying* and Elisabeth Kübler-Ross's *On Death and Dying*. As you might imagine, I wasn't much fun to be around, and I started spending more and more time by myself. Even though I had supportive friends and family, I shared little about what I was going through since everyone else seemed to have their lives figured out. I was going through a transition, navigating a Change Curve, but because I didn't know what to expect, I thought something was wrong with me.

My health eventually returned to normal, but parts of me *were* dying: my life and my identity as I knew them. I left my relationship, quit my job, and moved to Seattle, taking an interim job while I figured out what was next. Sitting in my crappy apartment one weekend, I dragged out the Joseph Campbell tapes and watched them all. As Campbell described the Hero's Journey, something clicked. I realized I wasn't hopelessly lost. More important, I knew I wasn't alone.

Connection Makes the Journey Easier

Knowing that we're not alone is powerful. I can't tell you how many times, in both my work and personal life, I've seen people shift their perspective when they realize they are not on their own—that others are going through or have gone through similar experiences to theirs. Their relief is palpable.

Remember the retreat attendees in chapter one who mapped their journeys? One of them told me later that she kept comparing herself to all the accomplished people in the room that day, questioning whether she belonged: "I have a tendency to look around and think everyone else has their act together. But I found out we were all dealing with something. . . . We all have our flaws, our bad days, and our doubts. . . . I learned I wasn't alone."

As humans, we're not designed to be alone. We are social animals whose well-being and survival depend on connections with others, and that need for belonging runs deep. If we feel excluded or rejected or that we don't measure up, the same areas of the brain are activated as when we experience physical pain. In other words, *rejection hurts*.

Feeling disconnected prompts us to view the world through a pessimistic lens. It makes us more likely to avoid the challenges in front of us rather than proactively addressing them, and our mental performance is likely to dip, leading to more mistakes and less creative thinking. Connecting with others helps regulate our nervous systems, reduces stress during big and small disruptions, and provides a sense of security when everything around us feels uncertain and heavy. As one of my clients put it, talking and sharing with other people "lightens the load."

Connection can also provide hope. One client told me that after being laid off from work, she had hope because other people believed in her. She essentially borrowed their optimism until she could believe in herself. Another woman who went through an unexpected divorce after twenty-one years of marriage told me it was her sister and close friends who helped her see there is life after endings.

Feeling connected with others can even alter our perception of a problem we're facing, making it seem more manageable. In a study conducted at the University of Virginia, researchers recruited volunteers on campus as they walked by, some of whom were alone while others were with a friend. One by one, the volunteers were told to put on a heavy backpack and stand in front of a nearby hill. They were then asked to look up the hill and estimate how steep it was. Those who had a friend with them thought the hill was less steep than those who were alone. (Those who had been friends with their companion longer thought the hill was even less steep).

The researchers then conducted a second study, this time at the University of Plymouth, with individual volunteers standing at the bottom of a steep hill. The participants who were asked to simply *think* about a close, supportive friend or relative perceived the hill to be less steep than those asked to think about someone they once knew well who had disappointed them.

This pair of studies offers an important takeaway: When supportive people are with us on the journey, even if they can't be there in person, our challenges don't seem as big.

A big proponent of connecting with others to make the journey easier is Patti Occhiuzzo Giggans, CEO of Peace Over Violence, a nonprofit working to stop violence against women and children. Patti and I first met in early 2019, when she was a guest speaker at a retreat on resilience that I facilitated. During her presentation, she stressed the importance of building resilience by building relationships. She encouraged everyone not only to take the time to develop both existing and new relationships but also to ask for help when they need it.

I've spoken with Patti a few times since that retreat, and I always love our conversations. She shared with me how challenging the pandemic was for her and that she needed extra support from not just family and friends but also peer and affinity groups. She did exactly what she had advised everyone at the retreat to do: she asked for help when she needed it. But her advice hit me differently this time, partly because I knew more about her. During her nearly eighty years of life, Patti has lived around the world, changed careers, earned a black belt in karate, been part of numerous social justice movements, and today is a well-respected nonprofit and community leader. I had unconsciously assumed that being such a strong person meant she didn't need much support from others. That couldn't be further from the truth. She stressed to me that she's able to be so strong *because* of her connections with others.

Build Your Support Crew

Who you surround yourself with has a big impact on you, your resilience, and your future trajectory. As several studies have shown, people's moods and behaviors can be contagious. You can "catch" someone's disposition like a common cold and start mimicking it without even realizing it. If you're around people who have a negative outlook on life or don't want to stretch themselves, you're likely to follow suit. If you spend time with people who are constantly growing and learning and are generally optimistic, their perspectives are going to rub off on you.

Be intentional about who you spend time with. As you connect with people who you resonate with and who care about you, you build what I call a "support crew"—a community of people you can turn to as you create your way forward.

There are three types of relationships in a support crew. *Core supporters* are the people with whom you have your closest, most caring relationships. *Travel companions* are people going through the same (or similar) experiences as you. *Guides* are those who offer direction and resources for your journey ahead. Sometimes, a single person plays more than one of these roles at a time—or over time. Some people may be in your support crew for decades while others may be in one of these relationships with you only briefly. Think of the people in your support crew not as set in stone but as more fluid, changing over time as your situation and relationships evolve.

CORE SUPPORTERS

The most supportive people in your life, those who are there for you during the ups and downs of your journey, are your core supporters. All of us need core supporters to keep coming back to throughout our lives as we explore, stretch, fail, and find a path forward. This kind of support isn't just critical during our formative childhood years; studies have also shown how important close relationships are in our adult years for continued development, resilience, health, well-being, and even for living longer. In one longitudinal study, adult development expert Marcia Baxter Magolda followed thirty-five young adults for more than twenty years. She found that one of the most important contributors to effectively navigating the ups and downs of their lives was having a secure base of relationships that both supported and challenged them.

Core supporters come in many forms: a close friend, a partner, a sibling, a parent, a mentor—anyone who provides that deep connection and support when we need it the most. As the word "core" suggests, your core supporters are just a few people, perhaps two to four. The number is small because it takes time and energy to cultivate and sustain close relationships. These relationships are almost always mutual—you are as ready to support each of them as they are ready to support you.

If you realize you need more core supporters in your life, your current circle of friends is a great place to start looking. Is there someone you'd like to build a closer relationship with? You can also seek out new friends you think might become core supporters over time. Either way, building a small, steadfast core group of supporters requires being proactive and intentional. You may be so busy with work and home life that investing time in friendships and core sup-porter relationships seems less of a priority right now. However, the effort and time put into those relationships is well worth it.

TRAVEL COMPANIONS

My friend Ray, whom I met at a leadership training nearly a decade ago, is incredibly warm and engaging and makes you feel like you're the only person in the room when he talks with you. But Ray told me he wasn't always like that. Growing up in Detroit in the late 1960s and early '70s, he learned that in order to survive, he had to keep to himself and not trust many people. It wasn't until he joined the U.S. Air Force after high school that he found the structure and stability he craved. And he found something else that mattered even more: a feeling of belonging he hadn't known outside his family before.

"It started with basic training," Ray said. "We all went through the same things. . . . Every day you had to overcome barriers lit-tle by little, so at the end, when you all graduated together, you understood that this is what community is about—this is what belonging is about."

Ray had found travel companions—people going through the same experience who wanted to support one another. Travel companions look out for one another, encourage one another, challenge one another, and hold one another accountable. While our core supporters may or may not know what we're experiencing (even as they care about us), our travel companions are right there with us. The shared experience builds strong connections.

When Patti Occhiuzzo Giggans, whom we met earlier in the chapter, reached out for support during the pandemic, she found travel companions in two places: a group of executive directors and an LGBTQ leaders' cohort. "That really helped me a lot because we were all in the same boat, trying to lead in the pandemic from home," Patti shared with me. She went on to name three ways these colleagues supported each other: processing shared challenges, brainstorming ideas together, and caring for one another. "We were all peers and had a common understanding of each other's challenges. We did calls on Zoom and really looked forward to it. You could feel the warmth and connection. . . . When someone was having an especially hard time, we'd focus on that person and let them know they weren't alone."

Travel companions don't always show up in the form of a group; in some situations, you might have a single travel companion—maybe a colleague at work or a friend or a sibling going through a similar challenge as you. However, the community generated in a group of people with a shared identity or experience is uniquely powerful because you're all traveling together.

GUIDES

While core supporters are the handful of people who are *for* you no matter what and travel companions are the people going through an experience *with* you, guides are the mentors, coaches, and others who provide counsel and tools to support you in moving forward. Typically, they are people who have been on a similar path themselves or, because of training or circumstance, can see your situation from a helpful vantage point.

Your relationship with a guide can be long term or brief. Sometimes, a single conversation or just reading about that person's journey can provide guidance or inspiration.

You also need different guides at different points in your career and life, and that may require proactively seeking them out. For example, you might email someone in a career or position that interests you as you explore what's next for you professionally. Or ask for advice from someone who has navigated a challenge, such as a health issue, similar to one you're facing. Or find another parent to talk to when you're feeling lost as a new mom or dad.

But sometimes the guide finds you.

When I was about to turn forty, I realized I was in the midst of a pretty big transition. I didn't know to what; I only knew I needed a change. Yet I felt stuck—I was in the Struggle part of the Change Curve.

I started having dreams that I had forgotten something. Initially, the dreams popped up sporadically. I would wake up with the sinking feeling that I'd forgotten something important and then wrack my brain: *Was it something at work? The kids? The hamster? When was the last time we fed the hamster?*

As time went on, the dreams occurred more frequently. At one point, I even sleepwalked, something I hadn't done since I was a teenager. I got all the way downstairs, where my night-owl husband was still awake, and started berating him about the important thing we had forgotten. He asked, "What did we forget?" At that point, I woke up—so frustrated at not being able to remember that I turned around and stomped back to bed.

What had I forgotten?

Soon after the sleepwalking episode, I attended a facilitation workshop. Having arrived early, I found a seat and then watched as others entered the room and got settled. A woman approached and sat down next to me. Eventually, we chatted about what we did for work, and I learned she was a coach. "I could use a coach right now," I said, and I asked for her card.

I decided to hire her. Before our first call, I pulled out a folder labeled "Coaching" that I had created back in my mid-twenties. During that prior transition, I had thought about going into coaching and even attended an information session for a coaching school. I had also considered writing a book. But I went another route and eventually got busy with work, got married, and started a family. I had let both these ideas go, thinking maybe I'd revisit them someday.

In that old folder were pamphlets from the coaching school and the business card of the person who had done the presentation. As I glanced at the card, I couldn't believe what I was seeing. My new coach was the person who had done that presentation fourteen years earlier. I sat in amazement at the chance of that happening. It still amazes me today.

My coach became a guide on my journey. Although she had shown up unexpectedly, I was ready. She helped me transition into the next chapter of my life and career. When I finally decided to pursue coaching professionally and to write this book, the "I forgot something" dreams stopped.

Ask for Support When You Need It

When you find yourself struggling with a problem, feeling lonely, or needing encouragement, reach out to your support crew and ask for help. Different people can support you in different ways, so as you choose who to connect with, consider the following:

What do I most need right now? Someone to

- *listen to me?*
- *help me brainstorm solutions?*
- *remind me that I'm not alone?*
- *give me advice?*
- *something else?*

Supporting Others Supports You Too

The body's instinctive response to fear is self-protection. And one of the best antidotes to fear is helping others. When you help others, lots of good things happen inside your body, including activation of the brain's reward system, the same one that turns on when you eat something delicious. In other words, *helping others feels good*. It releases neurochemicals that not only trigger feelings of pleasure but also make you less stressed and more optimistic in general.

In *The Upside of Stress*, health psychologist Kelly McGonigal writes, "When you help someone else in the middle of your own distress, you counter the downward spiral of defeat. . . . Helping others can transform fear into bravery, and powerlessness into optimism." She cites several studies that show how supporting others supports us too. For example, people who helped others after a natural disaster became more optimistic and energized, and people going through a life-threatening health crisis were more hopeful and less depressed after volunteering. Even small acts of kindness—offering a kind word or writing a note of appreciation—can have this effect.

While you may like the idea of supporting others, you may also be thinking, *I'm too busy putting out fires at work and at home. If I had more time for myself, I wouldn't be so stressed. Then I could think about others.*

As reasonable as that sounds, the results of a study on helping others and time might change your mind. Researchers from several top universities wanted to know what relieves the stressful feeling of not having enough time. As part of the study, they randomly split the participants into two groups, telling one group they could leave fifteen minutes early, giving them unexpected free time, and asking the other group to spend fifteen additional minutes helping edit student essays from an under-resourced local high school before leaving. Before exiting the study, both groups were asked to rate how much free time they had at that moment and whether they thought they had ample or limited time in general. Surprisingly, the participants who had helped others thought they had more time than those who had actually been given extra time. They also reported feeling capable and competent, which suggests that if we take time to support others, we may feel more effective at managing our own responsibilities.

Find Ways to Support Others

When you're feeling fearful, find ways to support others. Even small acts of kindness can have a big impact. The following are some ideas to consider:

- **Tell someone you're thinking of them:** If you have been thinking about someone you haven't talked with for a while, instead of keeping those thoughts to yourself, text, call, or send them a note.

- **Support a neighbor:** Check in with a neighbor who might need some extra help, and ask if they need anything.

- **Volunteer:** Consider volunteering, whether in the short or long term, for an organization or a cause that matters to you. This is also a great way to connect with new people.

- **Share appreciations:** When someone does something that you appreciate or that you admire, tell them!

- **Do random acts of kindness:** Give up your seat for a stranger. Pay for the coffee of the person behind you in line. Pick up trash on your walk. Smile at the people you pass.

However, while focusing on others' needs is a good thing, it's important to balance it with focus on oneself. Otherwise, well-intended generosity can turn into burnout.

Many people I work with are passionate about making a difference, and they give a lot of themselves to others. What sometimes surfaces, however, are twin hidden assumptions: that unless they are giving 110 percent all the time, they aren't doing enough, and that asking for help when they themselves need it is burdening others.

In fact, if you aren't taking care of yourself, you can't bring your best self to what you're doing. In the words of trauma expert Laura van Dernoot Lipsky, "We simply can't contribute skillfully and do our best work toward effecting external changes if we aren't also taking care of the place where overwhelm takes root: within ourselves." Being stressed and drained while you are doing good can inadvertently do harm since humans pick up each other's moods. If one person is anxious or panicking, the nervous systems of people nearby are likely to dysregulate, tipping them into a fight-or-flight state without their realizing why. Similarly, if someone is calmly assessing a difficult situation, others are likely to take on that demeanor too.

One more point about supporting others: When someone is upset or in a state of overwhelm, they may seek consolation and validation. Someone else, in their eagerness to offer support, may get caught up in the first person's problems such that the two together slip into "co-rumination," a spiral of mutual ruminating and problem-sharing that is hard to exit. For example, if one of your coworkers complains about another team member's low performance, and you chime in with your own frustrations about the same person, the conversation could become a laundry-list review of problems with that team member. The two of you end up stuck in what's not working rather than constructively addressing the issue.

How do we help ourselves and others fulfill the need for connection without co-ruminating, especially during tough times, when there is so much to commiserate about? Psychologist Ethan

Kross recommends listening closely to each other and acknowledging each other's emotions without getting lost in the story of what happened or might happen. While expressing feelings is an important step in processing them, it's equally important to eventually shift the focus to next steps. The practice of reframing discussed in chapter four can be useful here because it expands your perspective and reveals possible routes.

There is an art to connecting. It involves balancing your own and others' needs and processing feelings while also looking for opportunities to take action. Ultimately, whether you are the one giving or receiving support, the interaction isn't just about feeling connected; it's also about helping one another move forward.

FOR REFLECTION

- When you are facing change and uncertainty, who can you rely on to be part of your support crew? (Think about who is a core supporter, travel companion, or guide.)

- In what ways do you support others on their journeys?

- How do you find balance between focusing on others and focusing on what you need?

6

STAY CURIOUS

I wondered . . .

—DR. MAE JEMISON

Maya Shankar loved playing the violin. She started playing at age six, and at the age of nine, she was accepted into the pre-college program at the Juilliard School of Performing Arts in New York City. She spent the following years relentlessly practicing and performing and eventually caught the attention of renowned violinist Itzhak Perlman, who invited Maya to be his private student. Her big dream was to become a professional violinist, and she was well on her way to making it a reality.

However, when she was fifteen, while playing a difficult piece at a music camp, Maya overstretched a finger and suddenly felt a sharp pain. She went to specialists to figure out what had happened and was told that she had severely injured her hand.

Maya recalled, "Initially I thought, *I can beat this*. I refused to accept the injury and even tried to keep performing in concerts. But eventually, the pain got so intense the doctors said I really couldn't play anymore. And in some ways, that was a relief because I had been swinging back and forth between the highs of when I could play and the lows of when it hurt too much to continue. So when someone told me I had to quit, I finally had the decision that I didn't want to make myself. But I was, of course, devastated."

It was hard to let go of something that had been so integral to her identity, and Maya mourned the loss. She also worried whether she would ever find something else to be so passionate about. "I had been spoiled with that kind of passion," she said, "and it was going to be hard to acclimate to a world where I didn't get to feel that way."

That summer, while at home missing out on a concert tour, she came across one of her sister's old college textbooks while organizing the bookshelves in the basement. It was a book by cognitive psychologist Steven Pinker. She was curious. As she read, she became fascinated with how the mind works. She then spent the rest of the summer reading all the cognitive psychology books she could find. This new interest propelled her through the next decade, leading to a PhD in cognitive science and a postdoctoral fellowship in cognitive neuroscience.

When she realized she didn't want to be a professor, Maya began researching other options. That eventually led to her becoming the first behavioral scientist in the Obama White House, where she built a team to improve public policy across government agencies, and then the first behavioral science advisor to the United Nations. She had found another passion and really loved the work.

Then the administration changed, and she needed to find a new job.

Maya switched courses again. She wondered what a role would look like in an entirely new field, this time in the technology sector. "When you're thinking about next steps," she said, "sometimes those next steps are just not going to be readily available in your environment. . . . The path is not there, there is no path forward, and I took that approach again when it came to finding a job. I just refused to look at the cookie-cutter profiles for my skillset." Maya's unconventional thinking led her to a cross-country move and a new role working at the intersection of technology and human behavior, as well as eventually launching her podcast, *A Slight Change of Plans*.

"I do now feel like when one door closes, another one opens," Maya shared. "But the key is that it doesn't open without a lot of intentional effort and creativity. . . . I've tried my best to identify places where there could be an opportunity even if one doesn't currently exist."

As I listened to Maya's stories, I was struck by how she would allow time for processing each loss, yet, before long, her curiosity would have her scanning for what she could create next. At each transition point, she was able to let go of the past and refocus her energy and attention on the way forward. Maya has been quick to say she wouldn't be where she is without the support of many people. However, she also made those transitions successfully because she stayed curious.

A Certain Kind of Curiosity

When I started looking into the research on curiosity, I was surprised. I hadn't realized how many types of curiosity there are or how many theories exist about why we become curious. The two main kinds of curiosity, both of which are particularly relevant for navigating change, have been described by Dr. Judson Brewer, a neuroscientist and psychiatrist, as *destination* focused and *journey* focused. We'll call them "destination curiosity" and "journey curiosity." (These distinctions reinforce again the importance of the journey perspective when it comes to the creative way forward, which we also saw in chapter one and in Huang and Aaker's metaphor research in chapter four).

Destination curiosity is in play when we want to fill an information gap—right now. This is the curiosity you feel when you hear the ping of a text arriving on your phone. You might be doing something else important, but the curiosity of wanting to know who sent the text claims your attention, and that itch won't be scratched until you see who it is. This is also the curiosity you feel when searching online for an answer to a nagging question so you can move on with your day, or when a cliffhanger in a book or TV show is so compelling that you turn the page or click "next episode" on Netflix even though it's time for bed. In a nutshell, destination curiosity is about finding "the answer." Once you have the answer, destination curiosity turns off—until the next need-to-know surfaces.

Journey curiosity is the curiosity that drives us to explore and learn. It's the kind of curiosity Maya Shankar had when she came across the cognitive psychology textbook and then read whatever else she could find on the topic. As Dr. Brewer explains it, while destination curiosity is rewarding when you get the answer, with journey curiosity, the *process of being curious* itself is the reward. We keep going, wanting to learn more because it feels good. One of the best descriptions of journey curiosity I've come across is from Albert Einstein: "Most people stop looking when they find the proverbial needle in the haystack. I would continue looking to see if there were other needles."

We need journey curiosity to propel us through the twists and turns of change. Rather than getting tripped up trying to find "the answer" to whatever challenge we're facing, we need to be constantly learning—to be open to what's emerging and what's possible, since an answer that works at one point may not be the best answer going forward.

So what fosters journey curiosity? One of the most important tools for staying curious is asking questions.

The Power of Open-Ended Questions

Children are insatiably curious, coming up with endless questions about the world around them. In fact, research suggests that curiosity peaks around age four or five—and then declines. As they grow up, kids learn the "rules" of what works and what doesn't. As they become adults, they rely more and more on what they already know, or they become self-conscious about not having the answers, both of which make them less curious. And when people aren't curious, they ask fewer questions.

Asking questions is, in many ways, an art. Done well, it can reframe a situation and surface important information. In my work as a coach and consultant, well-timed, thought-provoking questions are among my most important tools. But it's not just any question that can unlock creativity. It's open-ended questions, in particular, that lead to new ideas and learning.

Open-ended questions can't be answered with a simple yes or

no. They typically start with "what," "when," "how," "where," or "why"—words that prompt the listener to think beyond a yes or no answer.* The power of this type of question is evident when the listener pauses to think more deeply, maybe even saying, "That's a great question" while contemplating an answer. To reframe a question in open-ended format, instead of asking, "Do you think this will work?" try "How do you think this will work?" Instead of asking "Did I do this right?" try "What did I do well, and what else can I learn?" Changing the question can change its focus and, very likely, the learning or outcome.

Ask Open-Ended Questions

Asking open-ended questions—questions that start with "what," "when," "where," "who," "how," or "why"—can surface new information, awareness, and ideas. The following are some open-ended question starters:

- What if . . .?
- What's possible now that . . .?
- How might we . . .?
- What's another perspective on . . .?
- What's important about . . .?
- Why is it done this way . . . and could we . . .?
- Where else could I look for . . .?
- What else might be true . . .?

---

* "Why" should be used carefully when asking someone other than yourself a question, since it can prompt defensiveness, leading to a reactive rather than creative response. To avoid this, be intentional when framing a why question. For example, clarify that you're asking "why" in order to understand the context or to generate new ideas.

However, open-ended questions can sometimes be more closed than open. For example, when you feel overwhelmed in the face of an uncertain situation—such as deciding what to do next after a layoff or after a long-term relationship ends—your curiosity may shrink to a single question: *What should I do?* Since it starts with "what," this seems like a good open-ended question, but it can actually keep you stuck in old frames and patterns instead of moving you forward.

In this case, it isn't the first word of the question that's the issue; it's the second word. Switch out "should" for "could."

Try it yourself right now. Think of an important decision you currently need to make or might need to make in the future. First, ask yourself, *What* should *I do?* Notice both what shows up in your body and the ideas that come to mind. Then, thinking about the same decision, ask yourself, *What* could *I do?* Notice if you experience anything different this time.

Typically, the "should" question prompts a restricted feeling in a person's body and thoughts about what they're "supposed" to do, while the "could" version of the question cues a feeling of expansiveness and more options in the mind. Shifting from the constrictive framing of "should" to the more open and exploratory perspective of "could" taps into your creativity and expands the range of possibilities you can see.

We can ask open-ended questions and pay attention to the words we use when framing them, but sometimes, we don't want to hear the answers. *Staying* curious means being open to the answers when they show up, even if they are not what we expected.

Journey Curiosity in Action

On the afternoon of January 15, 2009, Captain Chesley "Sully" Sullenberger got into the cockpit of US Airways flight 1549 to make a routine flight from New York's LaGuardia airport to Charlotte, North Carolina. It was bitterly cold outside as he and the first officer, Jeff Skiles, were cleared for takeoff. Their ascent began as on any other flight, but at almost 3,000 feet, the plane flew into a large flock of geese. The situation changed in an instant.

The birds hitting the plane sounded to Sully like heavy rain or hail. He heard them being sucked into the engines and could smell the burning. Seconds later, both engines failed. The plane decelerated. Then silence.

Sully wrote in his memoir, "Two thoughts went through my mind, both rooted in disbelief: *This can't be happening. This doesn't happen to me.*"

He quickly pulled himself out of that thought pattern, as he had only seconds to figure out what to do next. Noticing his body's reactions and the adrenaline rush, he was able to calm himself, becoming present enough to focus on the task at hand. He needed to find a place to land—but where? As he and Skiles talked with flight control and assessed the obvious options, Sully realized they couldn't make it to an airport runway. *What else is possible?* He could see the Hudson River below just to their left. While hardly ideal, it was wide enough and long enough for an emergency landing.

"I knew I had to solve this problem. I knew I had to find a way out of this box I found myself in," Sully said later.

He decided to go for the river.

In what was later called the "miracle on the Hudson," Sully

and his flight crew managed to not only land the plane in one piece but also get all 150 passengers and 5 crew members safely off the plane with the help of nearby boats before it sank into the near-freezing water. All this happened incredibly fast: only 208 seconds from the moment the birds hit the plane until the plane landed in the Hudson.

Sully credits his ability to land a commercial airplane in a river to his lifelong passion for learning. During his nearly thirty years as a commercial pilot, he had made a habit of poring over reports of flight accidents and descriptions of emergency scenarios just to learn more. In that crucial moment above the Hudson, all that curiosity paid off, helping him make split-second calculations and decisions. He believes that his entire life up to that moment had prepared him to handle the situation and save 155 lives.

Expanding Curiosity with Wonder

When the television series *Cosmos: A Spacetime Odyssey* came out in 2014, I was immediately hooked. At the time, I was juggling very full days of working, commuting, and raising young kids, and my long to-do list often left me exhausted. But every Sunday evening, as the wonders of the universe were displayed on the screen, from the evolution of life on Earth to the billions of suns and planets spinning in space, I would be reminded of the bigger picture.

Our daughter, Jackie, who was seven at the time, would sometimes join me, curious about what I was watching. During one episode, as we were being virtually swept across galaxies, she stared at the screen and simply said, "Wow."

Exactly.

"Wow" perfectly summed up what we were seeing on TV: We are mere specks suspended in a never-ending universe where everything is made up of stardust. *Stardust*. This cosmic dust provides the building blocks for everything: the food we eat, the cars we drive, the oceans and rivers, the most distant planets, and our own bodies. We're all made from the same stuff.

What Jackie and I experienced as we watched the show was *wonder*.

Wonder is powerful yet hard to define. There's "wondering about," which is what we're doing when we are curious, asking questions, and trying to learn more about something. The wonder I'm talking about, however, is "wondering at"—the awe or surprise that can open and broaden our perspective. It can be cued by so many things—looking up at the stars and remembering that each one is a sun, watching small creatures in a tidepool, hearing a baby laugh for the first time, witnessing an act of kindness, or being part of a team that achieves a significant goal. This kind of wonder makes us pause and notice.

While curiosity drives exploration and learning, wonder expands curiosity. The two work together in a virtuous cycle. The more we are curious, the more likely we are to experience wonder. And the more we experience wonder, the more we stay curious. Dacher Keltner, an expert on human emotions, has found in his research that experiencing wonder (which he calls awe) has a dramatic effect on our bodies, including reducing stress and encouraging us to be open and explore. When we feel awe, he explains, we see ourselves in the context of a much bigger, interconnected world, and our individual fears and challenges become smaller as a result.

Wonder also helps us see the ordinary in a new way. As one researcher describes it, "Wonder defamiliarizes the familiar, making it appear in a new light, as if seen for the first time." A perfect illustration is the *Cosmos* episode that explored what was happening within a single drop of water sitting on a bit of moss. At first glance, we see just a water droplet, but then we are shown the entire world within it, including tardigrades, or "water bears," swimming around. These tiny animals are incredibly resilient, able to survive extreme cold and heat. When there isn't enough water, they can suspend their metabolism for decades until conditions improve. I haven't looked at water droplets the same way since.

One of my favorite stories of wonder is about my friend Jeanette. After working as an attorney for fifteen years, she was ready for a new chapter in life, but she didn't know what that might be. Deciding to give herself time to explore and reflect, she quit her job in Seattle, moved out of her apartment, and backpacked for four months in Southeast Asia. While she was in Sri Lanka, she had a surprising cup of tea.

The tea was made from butterfly pea flowers. For centuries, this beautiful blue flower has been used in cooking and served as a tea not only for its health benefits but also because adding an acidic ingredient such as lemon to the tea turns the beverage from deep blue to a stunning purple.

When Jeanette added lemon to her tea and watched it change color, she was completely captivated. It was wonder in a cup.

"I remember being so delighted by this beautiful, color-changing tea," Jeanette told me. "A cup of tea is such a simple thing, but in that moment for me, it was a little bit of magic. . . . I could have had that same cup of tea hundreds of other times in my life, and I would have just guzzled it down and moved on. But this time, I wasn't distracted. . . . I was really open."

That cup of tea didn't just wow Jeanette; it got her thinking in a new direction. She wanted to share what she had experienced with others, so she decided to start an online tea business, naming it Waking Wonder. She'd never thought about being an entrepreneur before and didn't know where to begin, but now she was curious: *What might be possible?* There have been many ups and downs in launching the business, and Jeanette isn't sure where it will go in the future. "No matter what happens," she said, "I'm grateful for this experience."

Jeanette's encounter with the color-changing tea aligns with what researchers say happens during awe-struck moments. First, there is the feeling of *wow*. Something is so striking or novel— maybe a stunning vista, or someone's courageous act, or a beautiful tea—that it makes us pay attention. Then, our mental frames shift to accommodate this new information or experience. Monica Parker, author of *The Power of Wonder*, says this shift happens as "our brain tries to make sense of that *wow* experience, and our view of the world is different because of it." Similar to the reframing tools in chapter four, wonder changes our perspective, expanding our curiosity in new and different directions.

Look for Everyday Wonder

When you're busy and distracted, it can be hard to notice the wonder that, in fact, is all around you. Intentionally looking for "everyday wonder" keeps the curiosity–wonder cycle going. The following are some ideas:

- **Appreciate the everyday wonders around you:** Consider the wonder in simple things, such as water coming out of a spout, the design of a building, the alchemy of cooking, the taste of an apple, someone's kind gesture, or the funny things your pet does. Marine biologist and nature writer Rachel Carson used to ask herself, *What if I had never seen this before? What if I knew I would never see it again?*

- **Learn something new and interesting every week:** Challenge yourself to learn something new each week that's not work related.

- **Spend time in nature:** Nature, even in a small park or your yard, is full of wonder. Pay attention to the trees and how they move in the wind. Watch the sun set; it's never the same twice. If you live where it snows, catch individual snowflakes, and look at their intricate designs.

Imagining Possible Futures

When you travel where you've never been before, you likely use some sort of navigation aid, like a map or GPS. We twenty-first-century humans have become so dependent on these tools that many of us can't find our way without them. Consider what it would be like to get in a small boat with a few companions, with no compass or guide, and make your way across the largest ocean on Earth to a speck of an island you've never been to before and aren't even sure exists. Terrifying as that prospect might seem, that's exactly what ancient Polynesian sailors did more than a thousand years ago. They headed out into vast stretches of the Pacific, using the stars, sun, wind, clouds, waves, and currents to guide them to land they could imagine was there, even though they didn't know exactly where.

These navigators would literally feel their way along, sensing cues from the environment. They weren't relying on magic or luck; they were using navigating expertise handed down from generation to generation and honed through practice. With their ability to decipher subtle shifts in their surroundings, these voyagers were able to explore and discover new islands without maps or instruments, making them possibly the best navigators the world has ever seen.

What helped them do this?

Navigating without a map is made possible by a seahorse-shaped structure in the brain called the hippocampus. Let's say you're headed to a store you've been to many times before. Your hippocampus (along with other parts of the brain) accesses memories of the store and its location, essentially creating a mental map. You can make your way to the store on autopilot because that mental map is so familiar.

But let's say you miss a turn and wind up somewhere you haven't been before. You snap out of autopilot and start paying attention to the options in front of you: *Do I turn right, left, or keep going straight?* Before you choose, you try to anticipate each choice's outcome based on what you remember about the neighborhood: *Would this option get me closer to or farther away from the store?* This is also the hippocampus in action. It allows us to recall memories of past experiences and assemble them in different ways to imagine what might happen.

Besides helping us find our way on literal, physical journeys, the hippocampus also helps us imagine and navigate the future. For instance, you might be working on a project that hasn't gone as planned and is at risk of failing. As you try to come up with a way forward, your hippocampus searches your brain for relevant information—like a librarian doing a search, according to one neuroscientist—and combines bits of memory into various imagined futures. You consider these different options and then decide which one might save your project.

This is one of the superpowers of being a human: We can time travel in our minds to a future scenario, imagine what might happen, and then make a choice in the present based on that prediction. The Polynesian navigators didn't just navigate the Pacific Ocean; they *imagined* new places where they could go and then set out to find them.

So where does curiosity come in? Essentially, without curiosity, there would be no imagination. Curiosity primes the hippocampus, warming it up so we can absorb and remember what we learn. And because the building blocks of imagination are bits of memory, our view of the future is limited by our past—unless we bring in additional information. This is why staying curious about a broad range of things and learning from people with different experiences is so important: It supports our ability to come up with creative ideas for the future.

If you are facing a transition and need a new route forward,

Maya Shankar recommends that you "have many conversations with different people, read as much as you can, and watch as many movies and documentaries as you possibly can to broaden your view of what the world offers and where you as a person might be able to fit into that intricate web of possibility. Because it is very hard to come to terms with uncertainty when you are in a vacuum, and you just have your own mind to toss things around in. . . . It's important to be reminded of how much bigger the world is than the one you might have been occupying."

Imagining an array of possible futures—opening the mind, training it to look beyond right now and not be surprised by the unexpected—is fundamental to scenario planning, a process initially developed to help the U.S. military navigate the uncertainty of the Cold War. As the risk of nuclear war loomed and global politics escalated, the military needed to prepare for possible futures that had no precedent. So they imagined stories of what could happen and then determined possible responses to each one. While these scenarios were informed by current events and trends, imagination was required to come up with scenarios varied enough to cover a wide range of possible futures.

Scenario planning is now used by many organizations to prepare for uncertain futures. In its simplest form, it involves traveling various routes in your imagination and then coming back to the present day and choosing a way forward, knowing the future could unfold along any of those routes—or in some other way that wasn't anticipated.

This last point was emphasized by Sarah Chesemore, who did scenario planning on the future of global immunization at the Bill

& Melinda Gates Foundation. When I spoke with her at the end of 2020, she said, "It isn't really about the specific scenarios, though you would be surprised by how many elements of our 'least likely to happen' scenarios came true this past year. . . . It's more about stretching your mind. You can't predict what will happen, but if you have thought about it from enough angles, you are more prepared for whatever does show up."

Taking time to imagine the future is as valuable for individuals as it is for organizations. One simple yet useful tool is the Five Futures exercise. It guides you through imagining five possible futures for yourself, allowing you to dream a bit and then consider the impact of different scenarios. This process expands your perspective about the future and reminds you that there's more than one path forward.

Imagine Five Futures

The Five Futures exercise opens your mind to different future possibilities. It's best to write out your five futures in a journal or on paper rather than on a computer or tablet. Find a quiet place where you have space and time to yourself to do the first part of this exercise.

Imagine

- Imagine five *different futures* you would be excited about living. Give each future its own page, and on that page, describe what you are doing, feeling, seeing, and experiencing, as if you are currently living each future. Write in first person: *I am . . .*
- Let yourself dream. Don't edit yourself, thinking, *That's not*

continued

realistic or *I can't do that without a certain degree, years of experience, etc.*

- If you get stuck, think about what interested you at different points growing up. Perhaps there was a career you didn't pursue or a hobby you loved. What sparks your interest when you read books or watch movies? What do you enjoy talking about? What are other people doing that captures your interest?

Reflect

Once you've written about your five futures (it may take a few brainstorming sessions), set the writing aside for at least a week. Then, read through all five, highlighting any common themes and/or whatever stands out as interesting and exciting to you. Then, reflect on the following:

- What do you notice?
- What surprises you? What doesn't surprise you?
- Is there one future or a combination of several that seems especially interesting to you?
- Think about your preferred future within different future scenarios, such as an economic recession or boom, your industry thriving or struggling, or another pandemic or global health crisis. What opportunities and challenges might you need to navigate?

Staying curious expands our horizons and prepares us for whatever might be ahead. When we ask open-ended questions and don't assume we know the answers, we're more likely to learn something new. When we look for everyday wonder, we may be surprised by what we find, which in turn makes us more curious. And when we're curious about a wide range of topics and experiences, we're better able to imagine possible futures. In that imagining, we're inspired to explore, but it requires staying curious. A great reminder of this is the NASA project that sent a rover to Mars in 2011 to explore what might be a future home for humans. You know what they named the rover?

Curiosity.

FOR REFLECTION

- Think of times when you experienced destination curiosity and times when you experienced journey curiosity. How were they different?

- Try using more open-ended questions throughout your day. Does it make a difference? If it does, how would you describe that difference?

- When have you experienced wonder? What is something that made you stop and wonder at it?

7

IMPROVISE FORWARD

*Improvisation is the courage to
move from one note to the next.*

—BOBBY MCFERRIN

When you travel by boat on the Tanana River, you can't set out in a straight line, ignoring where the channels curve, without running your boat aground on a gravel sandbar. You also can't abandon steering and just flow wherever the currents take you without eventually getting stuck or running into something and capsizing.

The same is true in work and life. If you force your way forward without considering the changing context (and how you are changing), you will likely get stuck in old ideas. And if you just go with the flow without trying to influence where you are headed, you may end up somewhere you don't want to be.

This final practice—improvise forward—focuses on how we can creatively interact with our changing environment so we stay in motion. Like jazz musicians adapting as the music shifts, we improvise by creating with what's right in front of us. But we're not meandering aimlessly. We have a vision of where we want to go.

A Vision Moves You Forward

A vision is a picture of what we hope for in the future: where we want to go, what we want to do, and who we want to become. If that picture is inspiring and meaningful, it motivates us to keep going when the journey gets tough or when we realize how far we have to travel.

What makes a vision inspiring and meaningful?

The answer to that question lies in knowing what's core for you (chapter three). When your vision is aligned with your core values and strengths, you're inspired to work hard for it because it's important to you. Knowing what's core for you also helps you imagine what you want to see in the future. For example, when you brainstormed five futures (if you did that exercise in chapter six), your ideas didn't come out of thin air; they emerged out of what matters to you and what interests you.

The true power of a vision is not in the details of that future image but in the energy it creates. Research shows that people who have an inspiring vision feel optimistic and motivated. I can definitely attest to this. When I'm working with individuals or groups to imagine the future they want to create, the energy in those conversations is infectious, and I'm always inspired by them. Keep in mind, though, that if you're in the middle of a transition, imagining a new vision may be hard. It's okay if you don't have a clear vision yet. Just stay curious about what it might be.

Create Your Vision

This exercise is similar to the Five Futures tool in chapter six, but instead of exploring possible futures, you're identifying a vision that you want to commit to and work toward.

To create a vision, choose a future point in time—one, two, five, or ten years ahead. Then, imagine yourself fast-forwarded to that future moment. You are incredibly grateful for where you are, who you have become, and what you've accomplished. Finally, reflect on the following: What is happening? How is that future different from your current reality? Capture your thoughts in a journal, and identify one goal or next step that you want to work toward that's aligned with that vision.

When you do have a vision to work toward, there's a gap between where you are right now and where you want to be. To close the gap, you'll need to take a good look at the challenges you may encounter along the way. It might seem that thinking about challenges would be discouraging, but research by Gabriele Oettingen, a professor of psychology at New York University, has found the opposite. People who imagine both their vision *and* the challenges they need to overcome to make that vision a reality have better results than people who think only about their vision. When Oettingen's research subjects believed their vision was possible, exploring the potential barriers to it helped them get clear on what to do next and ultimately take action.

As you move toward your vision, however, you need to be ready to update it—or sometimes even let go of it. When you learn what works and what doesn't, you may realize that your vision is no longer viable or isn't what you want anymore. In *Emergent Strategy,* adrienne maree brown writes, "We can only see so far, literally and in our collective imaginations. So it's . . . good to be aware that you may be setting your vision based on the horizon you can see, and as you move towards it, it will change."

One story I love that demonstrates how important it is to be open to changing your vision comes from the tech sector. In 2011, Manny Medina and his partners launched the company GroupTalent with a vision of simplifying how corporate recruiters and job candidates find each other. They worked hard to make their vision a reality, but a couple of years into the venture, they were running out of money. As time ticked away, bankruptcy was looking increasingly likely.

In a final push to save the company, they created a sales tool to increase their personalized outreach and maximize their time. As Manny traveled around the country to meet with recruiters, he kept hearing no, they weren't interested in the services he was selling, but what was that sales tool he had used to set up the meeting? Manny started to wonder, *Is this a clue to the way forward?* He called his partners and pitched the idea of pivoting into a new business focused on sales software. The shift was risky, and everyone was tired, but they committed to the new direction. They convinced their funders to stick with them and rebranded the business as Outreach.

Manny and his partners let go of their original vision and began improvising their way toward a new one that was still taking shape. "When we made the pivot, we built software without knowing exactly what problem we were solving," Manny shared with me. "But we couldn't uncover the problem we were solving until we built the software." Manny knew the only way forward was to experiment—to be willing to fail, if necessary, and learn from those failures. He said, "You have to give it a turn; you have to be okay with being wrong and not lose faith."

The new product went through many iterations, what Manny called "micro pivots," before the company gained real clarity about their vision and how best to serve their customers. The effort paid off. Outreach has since become a "unicorn" in the start-up world, with a valuation of several billion dollars and offices around the globe. They succeeded not because they relentlessly pursued their original vision but because they were willing to change course when necessary and pursue a new vision.

Pace Yourself for the Long Journey

Ali Monguno, a Dubai-based architect, is also an adventure racer. He travels around the world with his teammates to navigate unmarked wilderness courses as they hike, climb, paddle, and cycle hundreds of kilometers to the finish line. Ali is known for his strong paddling skills and his adaptability when things get tough, which occurs often on courses like these, where unpredictable situations and extreme weather are the norm.

Whether he's working on his career aspirations or racing through the backcountry, Ali said he's learned a valuable lesson about moving toward a vision: the importance of pacing. To find the right pacing, one that will sustain him for the long distance, Ali has to adjust how he views each race. He has done the same with each career goal. "I've had to look at it as a marathon instead of a sprint," he said.

Whether it's a long race or a big vision, Ali shared that he paces himself by breaking the journey into smaller steps. He can then focus entirely on the next thing he needs to do. As he spoke, I was reminded of when I ran my first (and only) full marathon at age forty. The only way I completed it was by breaking everything down into smaller tasks and milestones: what I needed to do that week, that day, or that practice run as I prepared for the marathon. The day of the race, I focused on each mile, each water station, and the next time pretzels would be handed out. Each mini-accomplishment gave me a boost of energy to get to the next milestone.

Focusing on individual steps in the context of your bigger vision helps you bypass the fear reaction you may have when staring at a daunting to-do list or the yawning chasm between where you are and where you want to be. As you complete each action item, your brain releases dopamine, a feel-good chemical, which motivates you to keep going.

My client Deeann, a nonprofit CEO, shared, "When I'm overwhelmed by a big goal, I know I need to think about it in chapters, or seasons, or bite-sized chunks. I write down what's in my head so I can see the steps, and when I do that, my breathing slows down, I'm less agitated, and I can think better. I literally feel different."

Pacing yourself is also necessary when you don't yet have a vision, such as when you're deep in the bottom of a Change Curve, where everything can seem unclear and sluggish. In those times, you may not know what to do next, so focusing on small, positive steps becomes incredibly important. Maybe it's going for a walk that day, connecting with someone who can give you a new per-spective, or finishing a task that's been on your to-do list forever. In the process of taking small steps each day, stay curious (chapter six), and notice what seems interesting or where there's a little extra energy. These could be clues to your new way forward.

When you have a step-by-step focus, it also makes it easier to see when you need to adjust your level of effort. Ali Monguno told me that it's important to "be brutally honest with yourself about when you need a break but also when you need to push yourself harder." He recalled races and work projects where he overestimated how much he could do and then needed to adjust his approach so he didn't burn out trying to achieve unrealistic goals. But, he said, there are times when he does better than he expected, and rather than coast along, he pushes himself to take advantage of the surge in energy and momentum. No two races, projects, or days are the same, so it's important, Ali said, to focus on "one day at a time."

While there may be times when you need to take bigger, bolder steps to move forward, do not underestimate the power of pacing. It allows you to sustain your energy over time, adapt in the moment, and pay attention to what you need to do *right now.*

Manny Medina offered this advice: "If you make a little bit of progress every week, then you'll feel momentum going. The prog-ress doesn't need to be very material; it just needs to be there. . . . You don't need to kid yourself that you're going to hit the big home run this week; you just need to make progress this week. And it will be better than last week, and the week before that. . . . Commit yourself to that journey."

Pace Yourself

When you feel overwhelmed or stuck as you work toward a vision or a goal, try the following:

- Identify and focus on *the next small step* you can do today.

- Acknowledge and celebrate your progress as you go. Even the smallest steps can add up to big results!

- Take breaks. Vacations are important, but even if you can't take a longer break, try to play when you have time off, and schedule breaks during the day. (Take a break every ninety minutes—go for a walk, get a glass of water, stretch, etc.).

Manage Your Inner Critic

When someone pursues a new vision, they're likely to hear a lot of mental chatter. It's their inner critic trying to keep them safe by not moving forward or by playing small. It reminds them of all the things they have failed at or might fail at, how other people have done it better, or the debilitating catch-all: *You're not good enough.* The inner critic yammers at them for so long that it becomes the water they swim in, and the distinction between themselves and that voice blurs.

Practicing being present (chapter two) helps us recognize the inner critic, and then we have an opportunity to steer our internal dialogue into more useful territory. The following are some tools that help my coaching clients (and me) manage the inner critic:

Name the Inner Critic, and Set It Aside. The inner critic is not always a singular voice; there can be multiple inner critics. When you name the one that is speaking up, you're able to separate it out and mentally set it aside. *Oh, that's the naysayer critic again,* or *There's the judge. It's relentless today. I need to give it a break, let it go, release it into the river flowing behind me*—however you visualize releasing it. Naming something and reflecting on it allows us to see how it is distinct from us. Once we can see it, we can deal with it.

Challenge What the Critic Is Saying. The inner critic speaks in broad generalizations that usually prove false when they're questioned. For instance, when your inner critic says, "You can't make that work," challenge that statement by looking at it more closely. *What exactly am I trying to do that my inner critic says I can't? Why does it think it won't work? What information do I have (or can I get) to assess the situation? If the obstacles are real, how can I get around them?*

Explore the Worst-Case Scenario. If the inner voice is expressing worry, explore the worst thing that could happen. Staying curious, name your biggest fear about whatever you're trying to do. Sometimes further prompting—*and then what might happen? And what might happen after that?*—is needed to get down to the core fear.

When I take a client through this exercise, we talk about what they could do if their worst fear happened, what resources they could draw on. One of those resources can be remembering challenges they have moved through in the past—reminders of how resilient they are.

Talk to Yourself as You Would to a Friend. Another approach to managing your inner critic is to talk to yourself as if you're another person. Yes, really. Research by psychologist and neuroscientist Ethan Kross has shown that "distanced self-talk" has many benefits, including helping us shift from irrational to more generative thinking. It works by interrupting a negative chatter spiral, such as the one I experienced at various times while writing this book: *I can't believe I thought I could write a book. Who am I to write a book? What if the reviews are all one star? That would be mortifying . . . I shouldn't have started a book to begin with. I've wasted so much time on this thing.*

When you notice your inner critic, start talking to yourself as if you were your own guide or core supporter, addressing yourself by your name or as "you." Taking that perspective, here's what I would say: *Jen, everyone has doubts when they do something for the first time. Even if it doesn't turn out the way you hope, it will be a great learning experience. You know the material has already been helpful to so many people. By finally writing the book, you won't keep wondering "what if . . .?"*

This technique works because it creates an emotional distance between you and your experience that you naturally have between you and someone else's experience. "It's a lot easier for people to give advice to others than it is to take that advice [themselves]," explains Dr. Kross. "When you use a name to refer to yourself, it's almost like an automatic perspective switch. It's switching your perspective because you're so used to using these parts of speech when you address others." In other words, you aren't just talking to yourself anymore; in a way, you're advising someone else.

How we talk to ourselves has a big impact on what we think is possible and what actions we take. But we are not isolated from our environments. The broader social context we live and work within is full of negative messages, from institutional racism and sexism to social media images touting perfectionism and burnout culture. It's easy to internalize these outside voices, so as we work to create positive change around us, we need to learn how to shift from being our worst critic to our biggest supporter, especially as we travel in new directions.

Let Your Mind Wander (Creatively)

In 2006, Michelle Khine completed her doctorate in bioengineering and was excited to begin working as a founding faculty member at the brand-new University of California, Merced. However, she had a problem. To do her research, she needed specialized equipment to create fluid channels thinner than human hair on tiny biochips, but her new lab didn't have the equipment she needed. She was forced to improvise. "What brought me to the point of creativity was desperation," she said in a documentary on creativity. "After you've exhausted all of the known routes to get what you want, then you have to start thinking, *Well, what else can I try if I want to salvage my career?*"

Khine remembered a favorite toy from her childhood: Shrinky Dinks. Shrinky Dinks are thin plastic sheets you draw on and then heat in the oven to shrink them down to a much smaller size (I *loved* these as a kid). She applied that concept to her current challenge: She could create the chips she needed at a larger scale and then shrink them down. It worked. In fact, it not only allowed her to do the work she had promised; it also led to technological advances in her field and to her being named one of the world's top thirty-five innovators under the age of thirty-five.

Shrinky Dinks.

You can't plan this kind of stuff in advance. You have to trust that you'll figure out solutions as you go.

Improvising a creative solution, especially under the pressure of a deadline, can be tough to do. It may seem that applying more effort—"thinking harder"—will get you somewhere. Sometimes it does, but, counterintuitively, you're more likely to find inspiration when you stop focusing on the idea you're trying to come up with or the problem you're trying to solve.

Think of an aha moment that helped you move forward on a particular challenge. Did the idea pop into your mind when you were intently focused on the problem? Or did it happen while you were doing something else, like driving, taking a shower, or doing yard work? Based on research, there's a good chance that your creative idea showed up when your mind was wandering, not focused.

Letting your conscious mind wander allows your subconscious mind to make connections across different and seemingly disconnected domains or perspectives—in Khine's example, connecting a problem at work to a childhood toy. You're more likely to come up with interesting and unconventional ideas when your memory holds a broad range of experiences to explore and draw from. This is where the Stay Curious practice (chapter six) really pays off.

What you learn and discover today could lead you to the creative solution you need tomorrow.

It might seem confusing that I'm saying, "Let your mind wander!" after spending the entirety of chapter two ("Be Present") talking about focusing your mind. But the kind of mind-wandering I'm talking about requires that you are present enough to do it intentionally. First, you spend some time focused on the problem or opportunity in front of you. Then, you take a step back to give your mind some space to come up with a new solution or idea.

Generate Creative Ideas

Focus on the situation, problem, or opportunity in front of you, and ask yourself the following:

- *How is this like other situations I've faced?*
- *How is it different?*
- *What are possible solutions or ideas I can come up with right now?*

Once you've mulled it over for a while, put the problem and your reflections aside, and do something completely different. The ideas will be marinating in your unconscious mind, and insight may show up when you least expect it—even a few days later while you're commuting, showering, cooking, waking up from sleep, etc.

Dreaming is also a form of mind-wandering and can be a portal to creative ideas. For example, the Beatles' Paul McCartney said the songs "Yesterday" and "Let It Be" came to him in his sleep.

The inventor Thomas Edison would allegedly take naps with a pad of paper and pen next to him to capture the creative ideas that came to him during his dreams. Sleep expert Matthew Walker says, "Sleep provides a nighttime theater in which your brain tests out and builds connections between vast stores of information. This task is accomplished using a bizarre algorithm that is biased towards seeking out the most distant, nonobvious associations. . . . REM-sleep dreaming has led to some of the greatest feats of transformative thinking in the history of the human race."

When you're awake, however, letting your mind aimlessly meander for too long can result in rumination. You want to come up with a creative idea, but your mind wanders so far that you end up caught in a mental sweeper, rehashing the past or worrying about the future. If you find yourself doing this, take a few minutes to use one of the tools in chapter two, "Be Present," and then return to letting your mind wander (creatively).

The Art of Navigating Setbacks

In jazz and also in improv theater, a fundamental principle is to work with whatever shows up, creating a fluid continuity that's both ongoing and always changing. One of the core elements of improvisation is "yes, and." A jazz player recognizes what someone else in the band has played and builds on it. An improv actor kicks off a storyline, and another adds to it to keep the story going.

"Yes, and" is a useful perspective for navigating setbacks. When something doesn't go the way you planned, you can't change that reality. That would be like the guitarist stopping the saxophonist and saying, "Yeah, that didn't work for me; can you redo it?" Great jazz and great improv occur when the artists work with whatever is happening—even, and especially, when it's hard and messy. The key is acknowledging that the challenge, mistake, or loss happened and believing there is still a way forward if you look for it.

When the pandemic upended the restaurant industry in 2020, Maria Hines, owner of a James Beard Award–winning restaurant in Seattle, laid off employees and tried to stay afloat with a new takeout menu. As revenue plummeted, she tested a variety of other approaches, such as offering cooking classes and selling specialty items. She also found ways to cut costs, such as working without heat—bundled up in layers alongside her kitchen staff while preparing meals.

"'I *cannot* lose this restaurant. This is my life!'" she recalled to a *Seattle Times* reporter. "That's how I'd feel when I woke up, and I'd go to bed and I'd have that same fear—constant fear." But no matter what Maria tried, it wasn't enough. At the end of October 2020, she made the difficult decision to close the restaurant and go on unemployment.

Even then, she found new ways forward, including writing a cookbook and offering consulting and nutrition coaching. In an interview published in *The Seattle Times* one year into the pandemic, she said, "It's our creativity, it's our heart and soul that we're putting into whatever project we're in, so it's important that we remind ourselves that all that still lives within us."

The art of navigating setbacks includes deciding whether to keep going in a certain direction when we hit barriers and challenges or to let go and try something else. Sometimes, that choice is very clear or it's made for us, and other times, it's murky at best. While there's no single approach to making these decisions, it's useful to know how the mind can get in the way. For example, we have a cognitive bias called "sunk-cost fallacy," which is our tendency to want to stick with something we've already committed to, or invested time, money, or effort into, even when the cost of continuing outweighs the benefits. The sunk-cost fallacy is at work when people stay too long in a job, relationship, or project or persist after repeated setbacks when it's better to move on. The fallacy lies in focusing too much on the past when making decisions about going forward. The time or money spent so far is irrelevant; it's already gone. The question should instead be, *If I ignore everything I've invested or done up to this point, is it worthwhile to keep going in this direction?*

For Maria, the answer to that question was no. She knew she needed to make the hard decision to close the restaurant. It's not that she gave up. She kept going but in a different direction.

But sometimes the answer to the question is yes. Writing this book is an example.

In 2019, I committed to finally finishing this book after years of researching, thinking, and writing various versions—at times letting go of the idea only to find it coming back. I hired an editor in the fall, and we began to make progress.

At the end of that year, I needed a new computer, so I went to a store in the mall to trade in my old computer for a new one. Before wiping the old computer clean, the salesperson asked if my files were backed up to the cloud. I confidently said, "Absolutely!" since I'd been using a cloud service for years. We waited while the computer dutifully erased every file, flashing questions on the screen that essentially asked: Are you sure?

Yep, completely sure.

As the new computer downloaded my files from the cloud, my current files, including the book files, were not among them. I panicked a little, but the salesperson assured me the download would take time to complete, so I packed up my stuff and went home.

The next day, when I checked my computer, the book files weren't there. I logged directly into the files virtually. Still not there. Now in full panic mode, I asked my tech-savvy husband to check my computer, hoping he would miraculously find them. But they were gone. Every. Single. One.

It felt like a gut punch. I remember bending over, not really being able to breathe, as I realized that months of research and writing had been deleted.

Eighteen months prior, while traveling, I had worked offline. I didn't realize that my computer had never synched again to the cloud after I got home. During that year and a half, I had moved most of my book research and chapters into new folders. These were now gone. I was left with a few old book files and nothing else.

It took a few weeks to process the loss, with lots of tears, but eventually, I had to make a decision. I wanted to just walk away from the book. All that time invested in it seemed wasted. But that thinking kept me focused on the past. I had to decide if I was going to piece the book back together based on whether it made sense to write the book going forward.

I still believed writing the book was worthwhile, and I knew I'd regret not doing it, so I decided to start again. And in the process of rebuilding the book to what it is now, I realized something. The amount of information I had accumulated had bogged me down. With those files gone, I was forced to approach the book with fresh eyes. In the end, I believe I've written a better book than I would have if I hadn't given my old computer permission to permanently delete all my files. The setback turned out to be a gift in disguise.

One of the hardest things about a setback, and about change in general, is the feeling of having lost control. We make plans, and they don't pan out. We work hard, and the results don't match our effort. We go about our day-to-day lives and suddenly get broadsided by the unexpected.

We *want* control, but, in truth, we can control only some things, not everything. Identifying what we do and don't have control over and then figuring out what we *can* do is calming and supports focus. We swap rumination for action, which increases our sense of agency, our creative thinking, and, ultimately, our well-being.

Focus on What You Can Control

1. On a sheet of paper, create two columns with the following headings: What I Can Control, What I Can't Control.

2. Write down the things that are bothering you, sorting them into the two columns.

3. Notice what's on the What I Can't Control list, and mentally let it go. Identify one thing on the What I Can Control list that you want to take action on this week, and write down specific next steps.

Focusing on what we can control also helps us practice letting go, which is an important aspect of navigating change. We do our best on what we can control, but we let go of our expectations of how the future will unfold because we know the creative way forward is always fluid, dynamic, and often unpredictable. There will always be setbacks, failures, and detours, but they can be important pathways for learning and growth. We can also handle these challenges better than we may think—and research backs this up. We can say "yes, and," persisting on the course we've been traveling or finding an entirely new direction as we improvise forward.

FOR REFLECTION

- What vision are you currently working toward in your work or personal life? If none comes to mind, ask yourself, *What would I like to be different one year from now?*

- What obstacle might get in your way of moving toward that vision? What can help you navigate around or through it?

- How have you creatively navigated setbacks in the past? What did you learn that can help you going forward?

CONCLUSION

The future is uncertain. . . .
But this uncertainty is at the very
heart of human creativity.

—ILYA PRIGOGINE

As a kid, I loved the *Choose Your Own Adventure* books, in which you are the protagonist of the story and create your own narrative by making choices at certain points: If you decide to keep going forward, turn to page 28. Or if you decide to stay where you are, turn to page 20 . . . I would stay up late, returning to decision points and playing out the alternative choices, curious to see how each one turned out.

On one hand, this slight obsession has probably been helpful in my life and work because today I have a visceral belief that *there is always a way forward*. On the other hand, it's probably been unhelpful because it reinforced a false assumption of control. Because I got to see the result of every choice, I knew how each one would turn out. There was comfort in the certainty, and I wasn't left wondering what would have happened if I had made a different choice.

However, when it comes to making choices in the real world, with all its complexity, we can't know in advance how everything will turn out. The future is inherently uncertain, and there's no way to have all the information and to know all the answers. Yet it's precisely when we don't have all the answers that we often come up with more interesting routes forward because we're forced to get creative. So there is a paradox: As much as we may try to avoid uncertainty because it can be so challenging and disruptive, uncertainty, as Ilya Prigogine says, lies at the heart of human creativity.

That's the final thought I want to share in this book. The creative way forward requires that we embrace uncertainty, and to move forward in uncertainty, we need to balance contradictions and work with paradoxes. We can't get stuck in the "either/ors" and simple answers; we instead must be open to the "both/ands."

One of the contradictions to be balanced is between preparedness and adaptability—between thinking through and planning for possible futures in advance and being able to alter that plan in real time as the situation changes. Both are needed, but sometimes, we go overboard on one side or the other.

Early in my career and life, I leaned too far into planning, trying to control every outcome, similar to my approach to the *Choose Your Own Adventure* books as a kid. I learned over time, and continue to remind myself, that the purpose of planning is not to somehow predict or control the future; the point of planning is to prepare to adapt. When I facilitate group meetings and retreats, for example, I do significant planning beforehand, considering various approaches and how they might play out, and then the client and I choose an agenda. All that advance preparation allows me to adapt in the moment when it's clear that the group needs to shift directions or accomplish a goal in a different way.

Michelle Obama also talks about the dynamic between being prepared and being adaptable in her book *The Light We Carry*. She writes, "One of the greatest lessons life has taught me is that adaptability and preparedness are paradoxically linked." She has learned how planning, preparing, and practicing allow her to be more flexible in the moment when life throws its inevitable curves. "This helps me to operate with more calm under stressful circumstances, knowing I will most often, regardless of what happens, find some pathway through."

She goes on to say that "it helps if you're able to stay agile and adapt to change as it comes. And all of that becomes more possible, I've found, when you are *ready and practiced with a full range of tools*."

The practices and related tools in this book are designed for that purpose: to prepare you to be agile and adapt to the many changes ahead. Looking back over the practices in the past seven chapters, you may notice that some practices are opposites to each other, with contradictory approaches. That may look like a problem, but, in reality, it creates a dynamic tension that's part of moving forward creatively.

For instance, being present in this moment allows you to intentionally imagine what's possible in the future. Knowing what's core for you—who you are—provides a sense of comfort so you can stay curious about who you are becoming. And expecting a journey prepares you to work hard toward a vision *and* be flexible when things shift and evolve. At times, you may focus on one opposing practice more than the other, but to stay in motion, it's good to pay attention to how they work together and continually adjust to find the right tension between them.

One more pair of opposites to keep in mind on your journey is being optimistic about the future and acknowledging the reality, including the challenges, of what's happening right now.

I love the perspective Michael J. Fox offers on optimism. Fox is famous for his role in the 1980s sitcom *Family Ties* as well as many movies, including *Back to the Future*. He seemed to have a charmed life until, at age twenty-nine, he was diagnosed with Parkinson's disease.

Over the past thirty years, Michael's condition has progressed. He had surgery to remove a tumor on his spine, and when he could no longer reliably speak his lines, he had to give up his acting career. Even a simple action like picking up a glass of water or walking down a hall has required increasingly deliberate intention.

Through it all, he has sustained his signature optimism and humor. His optimism is not "toxic positivity," in which everything is rosy and nothing is wrong. He has faced and continues to face very real and difficult challenges. Instead, he says, "optimism is informed hope."

That kind of optimism—knowing what we're up against and still finding hope—is a necessity as we make our way into the future. There are no guarantees about what's ahead, and we can only speculate about the terrain we'll have to travel. But we *can* build our capacity to creatively adapt in the uncertainty.

As you go through the ups and downs and twists and turns of your journey, my hope is that this guidebook will remind you that you're not alone and that no matter what happens, there is always a way forward.

TOOLS FOR NAVIGATING CHANGE

ACKNOWLEDGMENTS

There were so many points during the writing of this book when I wanted to stop and just let it go, but it wouldn't let go of me. It was an incredible amount of work that often left me exhausted, humbled, and wondering what the hell I was doing. But there were also times of deep learning, heartfelt connections, and gratitude. In many ways, it was like going through a long transition, and while I've grown a lot in the process, I'm glad I'm on the other side (at least for now).

During my research, I learned that a common definition of creativity is taking what's available and putting it together in a new and different way that is useful. The lessons in this book are drawn from so many before me whom I have learned from over the years—either directly or by reading their books and research. My hope is that I've put the information together in a new and different way that will help readers navigate change creatively. I know time is one of our most precious resources, so thank you for spending some of it with me.

This book would not have been possible without so many people:

First, to my clients, thank you for trusting me over the years to support you in your growth and development in this ever-changing world. Your partnership has been a gift, and I've learned so much from working with each of you.

To everyone who shared your time and stories with me for this book, I can't tell you how much I appreciate you and the lessons you've shared. This book wouldn't have been possible without you.

To my long-time editor, Carolyn Bond, you are much more than an editor. Friend, therapist, champion, truth-teller—thank you for your sharp editorial eye, your patience, and your flexibility with all my e-mails that began, "I was thinking . . ."

Thank you to the hard-working and talented editors, designers, project managers, and marketers at Greenleaf Book Group and Fast Company Press: Aaron, Benito, Jeanette, John, Kyle, Madelyn, Morgan, Steve, and Tiffany.

Thank you to all of you who were a sounding board, a reader, and a champion for all these years. Some of you were involved so far back with earlier iterations that you probably forgot I was writing a book. In particular, thank you to Amy, Bo, Cindy, Deeann, Emily, Heather, Jennifer, Julie, Justin, Kelli, Kristen, Lucy, Marshall, Meghan, Melanie, Mike, Natalie, Paul, Ray, Shelly, Sophia, Sue, and Virginia. Gina, thank you for the beautiful drawings of the Tanana River and Healy Lake. Jessie, thank you for sharing your stunning photo for the cover! Jeanette, thank you for being the first reader. I still remember asking you, "Who am I to write a book?" and your wonderful response of "Why not you?"

To my family, thank you for your support, especially when I took my various leaps of faith over the years. Jackie and Ian, I hope you go into the world knowing that you are loved SO much and that the curves are part of the journey.

Finally, to Chip, I could not have dreamed up a better partner and am looking forward to many more adventures. Thank you for your constant encouragement, as well as your humor, love, and openness to taking risks. As you said, we're "Team Martin," and we'll figure it out together, no matter what's ahead.

NOTES

EPIGRAPH

viii   **"To exist is to change . . ."**: Henri Bergson, *Creative Evolution* (New York: Dover Publications, 1998), 7.

INTRODUCTION

1   **"The river moves . . ."**: Kekla Magoon, *The Rock and The River* (New York: Aladdin, 2010), 283.

3   **"If you try to hold on to some stable identity . . ."**: Yuval Noah Harari, *21 Lessons for the 21st Century* (New York: Spiegel & Grau, 2018), 269 and 266.

4   **global surveys of leaders**: Alex Gray, "The 10 Skills You Need to Thrive in the Fourth Industrial Revolution," World Economic Forum, January 19, 2016, https://www.weforum.org/agenda/2016/01/the-10-skills-you-need-to-thrive-in-the-fourth-industrial-revolution/; "Capitalizing on Complexity: Insights from the Global Chief Executive Officer Study," IBM, 2010, https://public.dhe.ibm.com/software/it/events/smartwork/pdf/Public_Ex_Summary.pdf.

4   **when we most need to be creative**: My understanding of the creative–reactive dynamic has been influenced by Bob

Anderson (www.leadershipcircle.com) and Dr. Dan Siegel (www.drdansiegel.com).

4   **your mind**: Daniel J. Siegel, *Aware: The Science and Practice of Presence* (New York: TarcherPerigee, 2018), 44. There are many different opinions and definitions of what exactly the "mind" is. Dr. Daniel Siegel describes the mind as "the embodied and relational, emergent self-organizing process that regulates the flow of energy and information."

5   **you can't step into the same river twice**: Roger von Oech, *Expect the Unexpected or You Won't Find It: A Creativity Tool Based on the Ancient Wisdom of Heraclitus* (San Francisco: Berrett-Koehler, 2002), 49–54.

6   **research and science behind why it works**: Notably, much of the published behavioral and psychological research is based on small samples from WEIRD societies (Western, Educated, Industrialized, Rich, and Democratic). Where possible, I've included multiple studies, as well as stories and perspectives of people with different identities, backgrounds, and experiences.

CHAPTER 1

7   **"The journey, not the . . ."**: While commonly attributed to T. S. Eliot, the exact source is unknown.

9   **"You can get stuck in thinking . . ."**: 2016–17 leadership program participant, interview with author, February 6, 2020.

10   **forms a sigmoid curve, or "S-curve"**: The S-curve

framework is used to represent the growth and decline of not just living systems but of many different things, such as new product or technology adoption.

10   **"The secret to constant growth . . ."**: Charles Handy, *The Age of Paradox* (Boston: Harvard Business School Press, 1995), 53. See also: Juan Carlos Méndez-García and Whitney Johnson, "Throw Your Life a Curve," *Harvard Business Review,* September 3, 2012, accessed online March 22, 2021, https://hbr.org/2012/09/throw-your-life-a-curve/. Juan Carlos Méndez-García and Whitney Johnson have applied the S-curve concept to careers, noting that people need to embrace jumping to a new S-curve to continually grow and learn.

11   **we also go through an internal transition**: William Bridges, *Transitions: Making the Most of Life's Changes,* 2nd ed. (Cambridge: Da Capo Press, 2004), xii–xiii. William Bridges made a distinction between "change" (the event or situation that is different) and "transition" (the internal psychological processing people go through to accept and integrate that change). While I find his distinction helpful, I don't strictly follow his word choices in this book. For example, "going through change" can refer to both the external shift and the internal transition.

11   **Elisabeth sat across the desk**: Elisabeth Kübler-Ross, *The Wheel of Life: A Memoir of Living and Dying* (New York: Touchstone, 1998), 109–113. This version of Elisabeth's story is drawn from her account in her memoir.

12   **Wanting to help people face**: Lucy Burns, "Elisabeth

Kübler-Ross: The Rise and Fall of the Five Stages of Grief," BBC News, July 3, 2020, accessed online September 1, 2021, https://www.bbc.com/news/stories-53267505/.

12   **Elisabeth believed this information could also be useful**: Elisabeth Kübler-Ross, *Death: The Final Stage of Growth* (New York: Simon & Schuster, 1975), 145.

13   **While there is no perfect model**: Models like the Five Stages model have been criticized for implying that everyone goes through the same linear, stage-by-stage process, which isn't true. Models and frameworks aren't meant to be pre-scriptive; they serve as general maps, helping us to reflect upon and understand our experiences.

13   **my own version of the Change Curve**: Bridges, *Transitions*; William Bridges, *Managing Transitions: Making the Most of Change*, 3rd ed. (Boston: Da Capo Press, 2009); Elisabeth Kübler-Ross, *On Death and Dying: What the Dying Have to Teach Doctors, Nurses, Clergy and Their Own Families* (New York: Scribner, 1969); Robert Kegan, *The Evolving Self: Problem and Process in Human Development* (Cambridge: Harvard University Press, 1982); Handy, *The Age of Paradox*; Margaret J. Wheatley, *Leadership and the New Science: Discovering Order in a Chaotic World* (San Francisco: Berrett-Koehler Publishers, Inc., 2006); C. Otto Scharmer, *Theory U: Leading from the Future as It Emerges* (San Francisco: Berrett-Koehler Publishers, Inc., 2009); Frederic M. Hudson, *The Adult Years: Mastering the Art of Self-Renewal* (San Francisco: Jossey-Bass, 1999); Joseph Campbell, *The Hero with a Thousand Faces*, 3rd ed.

(Novato: New World Library, 2008). My Change Curve version is informed by my coaching and consulting work, as well as these resources.

15   **We feel the pain of the loss more**: Daniel Kahneman, *Thinking Fast and Slow* (New York: Farrar, Straus and Giroux, 2013), 283–309.

15   **"Here is a river . . ."**: Margaret J. Wheatley, *Perseverance* (San Francisco: Berrett-Koehler, 2010).

16   **while inwardly feeling as if in a blank space**: Bridges, *Transitions*, 133–155. This is what William Bridges calls the "neutral zone."

16   **the caterpillar's imaginal cells**: Ferris Jabr, "How Does a Caterpillar Turn into a Butterfly?" *Scientific American*, August 10, 2012, accessed online September 1, 2021, https://www.scientificamerican.com/article/caterpillar -butterfly-metamorphosis-explainer/.

20   **"Until one is committed . . ."**: W. H. Murray, *The Scottish Himalayan Expedition* (London: J. M. Dent & Sons, 1951), 6–7.

22   **"A map is not the territory . . ."**: Alfred Korzybski, *Selections from Science and Sanity: An Introduction to Non-Aristotelian Systems* and *General Semantics*, 2nd ed. (New York: Institute of General Semantics, 2010), 24.

22   **people spend almost half their adult lives**: Daniel J. Levinson, *The Seasons of a Woman's Life* (New York: Alfred A. Knopf, 1996), 25; Bruce Feiler, *Life is in the Transitions: Mastering Change at Any Age* (New York: Penguin Press, 2020), 16.

CHAPTER 2

25   **"Be still like a mountain, and flow..."**: While commonly attributed to Lao Tzu, the exact source is unknown.

26   **According to research**: Amishi P. Jha, "Being in the Now," *Scientific American Mind* 24, no. 1 (February 2013): 26–33, DOI: 10.1038/scientificamericanmind0313-26; Amishi P. Jha, *Peak Mind: Find Your Focus, Own Your Attention, Invest 12 Minutes a Day* (New York: HarperCollins, 2021).

26   **In this distracted state**: Jha, "Being in the Now"; Jessica Stillman, "New Study: Multitasking Is Making Your Anxiety Worse," *Inc.*, May 27, 2020, accessed July 10, 2021, https://www.inc.com/jessica-stillman/new-study-multitasking-is-making-your-anxiety-worse.html/; Matthew A. Killingsworth and Daniel T. Gilbert, "A Wandering Mind Is an Unhappy Mind," *Science* 330, no. 6006 (November 2010): 932, DOI: 10.1126/science.1192439.

27   **what's often called mindfulness**: Jon Kabat-Zinn, *Full Catastrophe Living: Using the Wisdom of Your Body and Mind to Face Stress, Pain, and Illness* (New York: Bantam Books, 2013), xxxv. Researchers have different interpretations of what mindfulness means, but a general definition is being in the present moment without judgment.

27   **numerous studies have shown**: Jha, "Being in the Now"; Laura G. Kiken and Natalie J. Shook, "Looking Up: Mindfulness Increases Positive Judgements and Reduces Negativity Bias," *Social Psychological and Personality Science* 2, no. 4 (January 2011): 425–431, DOI:

10.1177/1948550610396585; Adam Moore and Peter Malinowski, "Meditation, Mindfulness and Cognitive Flexibility," *Conscious and Cognition* 18, no. 1 (March 2009): 176–186, DOI: 10.1016/j.concog.2008.12.008; Emma Schootstra, Dirk Deichmann, and Evgenia Dolgova, "Can 10 Minutes of Meditation Make You More Creative?," *Harvard Business Review*, August 29, 2017, accessed online August 2, 2021, https://hbr.org/2017/08/can-10-minutes-of-meditation-make-you-more-creative/; Daniel Goleman and Richard J. Davidson, *Altered Traits: Science Reveals How Meditation Changes Your Mind, Brain, and Body* (New York: Avery, 2017).

27   **you are a firefighter**: Norman Maclean, *Young Men and Fire* (Chicago: The University of Chicago Press, 1992). This scenario is adapted from the Mann Gulch Fire tragedy as described by Norman Maclean.

28   **they would have survived**: David Epstein, *Range: Why Generalists Triumph in a Specialized World* (New York: Riverhead Books, 2019), 245–247.

29   **what has worked in the past**: Karl E. Weick, "The Collapse of Sensemaking in Organizations: The Mann Gulch Disaster," *Administrative Science Quarterly* 38, no. 4 (December 1993): 628–652, DOI: 10.2307/2393339; Karl E. Weick, "Drop Your Tools: On Reconfiguring Management Education," *Journal of Management Education* 31, no. 1 (February 2007): 5–16, DOI: 10.1177/1052562906293699.

29   **come up with this counterintuitive idea**: Maclean, *Young Men and Fire*, 74–105. Escape fires had been used

before then, but Dodge said he had no prior knowledge of them.

30   **She has found**: Amishi P. Jha et al., "Short-Form Mindfulness Training Protects Against Working Memory Degradation over High-Demand Intervals," *Journal of Cognitive Enhancement* 1, no. 2 (June 2017): 154, DOI: 10.1007/s41465-017-0035-2; Barry Yeoman, "Training the Brains of Warriors," Mindful, July 3, 2019, accessed online July 10, 2021, https://www.mindful.org/training-the-brains-of-warriors/; Ekaterina Denkova et al., "Is Resilience Trainable? An Initial Study Comparing Mindfulness and Relaxation Training in Firefighters," *Psychiatry Research* 285, no. 1 (January 2020): 112794, DOI: 10.1016/j.psychres.2020.112794.

30   **when we perceive we are in danger**: Robert M. Sapolsky, *Behave: The Biology of Humans at our Best and Worst* (New York: Penguin Books, 2018), 31–44; "Understanding the Stress Response," Harvard Medical School, July 6, 2020, accessed online July 23, 2021, https://www.health.harvard.edu/staying-healthy/understanding-the-stress-response/. The amygdala (or amygdalae, since there are two) works with other parts of the brain to determine what we should pay attention to in any given moment. It prioritizes novelty and uncertainty. When it registers something as dangerous, the amygdala sends a signal to the hypothalamus, activating the sympathetic nervous system, which in turn prepares us for fight or flight to protect ourselves.

Bessel Van Der Kolk, *The Body Keeps the Score: Brain,*

Mind, and Body in the Healing of Trauma (New York: Viking, 2014), 80–83; Leon F. Seltzer, "Trauma and the Freeze Response: Good, Bad, or Both?" *Psychology Today*, July 8, 2015, accessed online September 4, 2020, https://www.psychologytoday.com/us/blog/evolution-the-self/201507/trauma-and-the-freeze-response-good-bad-or-both. When we perceive extreme danger and can't protect ourselves by fighting or fleeing, our bodies may "freeze."

Gina Ryder, "The Fawn Response: How Trauma Can Lead to People-Pleasing," PsychCentral, January 10, 2022, accessed online November 6, 2023, https://psychcentral.com/health/fawn-response#types-of-trauma/. A fourth threat or trauma response, sometimes called "fawn," is when we try to please or appease others to stay safe.

Shelley E. Taylor et al., "Biobehavioral Responses to Stress in Females: Tend-and-Befriend, Not Fight-or-Flight," *Psychological Review* 107, no. 3 (July 2000): 411–429, DOI: 10.1037/0033-295x.107.3.411. In 2000, a theory was proposed that females have more of a "tend and befriend" stress response after noting the original research on fight or flight was done predominantly on male rats.

30 **less access to our prefrontal cortex**: Daniel J. Siegel, *Mindsight: The New Science of Personal Transformation* (New York: Bantam Books, 2011), 21–37; Ronald S. Friedman and Jens Förster, "The Effects of Promotion and Prevention Cues on Creativity," *Journal of Personality and Social Psychology* 81, no. 6 (December 2001): 1001–1013, DOI:

10.1037/0022-3514.81.6.1001; Arne Dietrich, "The Cognitive Neuroscience of Creativity," *Psychonomic Bulletin & Review* 11, no. 6 (December 2004): 1011–1026, DOI: 10.3758/bf03196731; David Rock, *Your Brain at Work: Strategies for Overcoming Distraction, Regaining Focus, and Working Smarter All Day Long* (New York: Harper Business, 2009), 108–111.

30   **"It's like doing a core workout . . ."**: Maggie Seaver, "What Mindfulness Does to Your Brain: The Science of Neuroplasticity," *Real Simple*, October 1, 2020, accessed online July 7, 2021, https://www.realsimple.com/health/mind-mood/mindfulness-improves-brain-health-neuroplasticity/.

31   **Dr. Amishi Jha's research shows**: Jha, *Peak Mind*, 272–276. Dr. Jha's research shows the "minimum required dosage" to experience the benefits of meditation is twelve minutes a day, five days a week, for four weeks.

32   **one of the fastest ways to feel calmer**: Alice Park, "This is the Fastest Way to Calm Down," *TIME*, March 30, 2017, accessed online August 10, 2021, https://time.com/4718723/deep-breathing-meditation-calm-anxiety/; David DiSalvo, "How Breathing Calms Your Brain," *Psychology Today*, December 31, 2017, accessed online July 30, 2021, https://www.psychologytoday.com/us/blog/neuronarrative/201712/how-breathing-calms-your-brain/.

32   **Breathing is one of the few**: Van Der Kolk, *The Body Keeps the Score*, 64.

34   **a long-time client**: Natalie, interview with author, July 9, 2021. All quotes from Natalie are from that interview.

35   **as the late Sir Ken Robinson joked**: Sir Ken Robinson, "Do Schools Kill Creativity?" TED Talk, February 2006, 19:11, accessed online August 3, 2021, https://www.ted.com/talks/sir_ken_robinson_do_schools_kill_creativity/.

37   **scientists in Israel conducted a study**: Lisa Feldman Barrett, *How Emotions Are Made: The Secret Life of the Brain* (New York: Mariner Books, 2018), 73–75; Shai Danziger, Jonathan Levav, and Liora Avnaim-Pesso, "Extraneous Factors in Judicial Decisions," *Proceedings of the National Academy of Sciences of the United States of America* 108, no. 17 (April 2011): 6889–6892, DOI: 10.1073/pnas.1018033108.

37   **While scientists debate**: Julie Beck, "Hard Feelings: Science's Struggle to Define Emotions," *The Atlantic*, February 24, 2015, accessed online July 15, 2021, https://www.theatlantic.com/health/archive/2015/02/hard-feelings-sciences-struggle-to-define-emotions/385711/. This is a good summary of different perspectives on emotions.

38   **how you feel about it informs your decision**: David Eagleman, *The Brain: The Story of You* (New York: Vintage Books, 2017), 119–128; Daniel Gilbert, *Stumbling on Happiness* (New York: Vintage Books, 2007), 130–135.

38   **Without that emotional input**: Sapolsky, *Behave*, 54–58.

38   **If you are anxious**: Gilbert, *Stumbling on Happiness*, 134–138.

38   **Even the weather can affect how you're feeling**: Gilbert, *Stumbling on Happiness*, 136.

38   **buffalo on the Great Plains**: "Facing the Storm: Story of the American Bison," Big Sky Pictures, High Plains Film, Montana Public Television, 2010, http://www.highplains-films.org/films/facing_the_storm; Jim Matheson, email messages to author, February 2020. Jim Matheson, executive director of the National Bison Association, shared with me the behaviors of cattle and buffalo in storms.

39   **naming emotions regulates emotional responses**: Barrett, *How Emotions Are Made*, 120–124; Jared B. Torre and Matthew D. Lieberman, "Putting Feelings into Words: Affect Labeling as Implicit Emotion Regulation," *Emotion Review* 10, no. 2 (March 2018): 116–124, DOI: 10.1177/1754073917742706; Matthew D. Lieberman et al., "Subjective Responses to Emotional Stimuli during Labeling, Reappraisal, and Distraction," *Emotion* 11, no. 3 (June 2011): 468–480, DOI: 10.1037/a0023503; Susan David, "3 Ways to Better Understand Your Emotions," *Harvard Business Review*, November 10, 2016, accessed online July 28, 2021, https://hbr.org/2016/11/3-ways-to-better-understand-your-emotions/.

39   **In a study done at UCLA**: Matthew D. Lieberman et al., "Putting Feelings into Words: Affect Labeling Disrupts Amygdala Activity in Response to Affective Stimuli," *Psychological Science* 18, no. 5 (May 2007): 42–428, DOI: 10.1111/j.1467-9280.2007.01916.x/.

39   **"When you put feelings into words . . ."**: Stuart Wolpert, "Putting Feelings into Words Produces Therapeutic Effects in the Brain: UCLA Neuroimaging Study Supports Ancient

Buddhist Teachings," UCLA Newsroom, June 21, 2007, accessed online July 30, 3021, https://newsroom.ucla.edu/releases/Putting-Feelings-Into-Words-Produces-8047/.

39   **research shows that using more specific emotional language**: Todd B. Kashdan, Lisa F. Barrett, and Patrick E. McKnight, "Unpacking Emotion Differentiation: Transforming Unpleasant Experience by Perceiving Distinctions in Negativity," *Current Directions in Psychological Science* 24, no. 1 (February 2015): 10–16, DOI: 10.1177/0963721414550708; Michele M. Tugade, Barbara L. Frederickson, and Lisa Feldman Barrett, "Psychological Resilience and Positive Emotional Granularity: Examining the Benefits of Positive Emotions on Coping and Health," *Journal of Personality* 72, no. 6 (December 2004): 1161–1190, DOI: 10.1111/j.1467-6494.2004.00294.x/.

41   **rather than getting caught up**: Timothy D. Wilson, *Redirect: Changing the Stories We Live By* (New York: Back Bay Books, 2015), 5–6. While it can be helpful to journal or talk with others about your experiences—the story of what has happened—there is also research showing that talking about a traumatic event right after it occurs can make the person relive the event and solidify that memory. Letting some time pass before reflecting on an experience may be helpful.

CHAPTER 3

43   **"From Starfish I have learned . . .":** JoLillian T. Zwerdling quoted in adrienne maree brown, *Emergent Strategy: Shaping Change, Changing Worlds* (Chico: AK Press, 2017), 124.

44   **One photo series:** "Sea Star Wasting Syndrome," UC Santa Cruz, accessed online, September 11, 2020, https:// marine.ucsc.edu/data-products/sea-star-wasting/.

44   **These starfish were still:** Austin Price, "Left for Dead, Starfish Bounce Back: Genetic Resilience in the Face of Astronomical Die-Off," *Sierra*, September 29, 2018, accessed online September 11, 2020, https://www. sierraclub.org/sierra/left-for-dead-starfish-bounce-back; Lauren M. Schiebelhut, Jonathan B. Puritz, and Michael N. Dawson, "Decimation by Sea Star Wasting Disease and Rapid Genetic Change in a Keystone Species, *Pisaster Ochraceus*," *Proceedings of the National Academy of Sciences of the United States of America* 115, no. 27 (June 2018): 7069–7074, DOI: 10.1073/pnas.1800285115.

44   **Ilya Prigogine discovered:** Margaret J. Wheatley, *Leadership and the New Science: Discovering Order in a Chaotic World* (San Francisco: Berrett-Koehler Publishers, 2006), 20–21; Margaret J. Wheatley, "Chaos and Complexity: What Can Science Teach?" *OD Practitioner*, Fall 1993, 6, https:// www.margaretwheatley.com/articles/Wheatley-Chaos-and -Complexity.pdf; Marjorie Kelly, "Taming the Demons of Change: When Chaos Turns Out to Be an Angel in Disguise," *Business Ethics*, July/August 1993, 6–7, https://marjoriekelly.

org/wp-content/uploads/2021/09/Vol07No04Tamingthe DemonsofChange.pdf; Mihaly Csikszentmihalyi, *Flow: The Psychology of Optimal Experience* (New York: Harper Perennial Modern Classics, 2008), 201; Renée Weber, *Dialogues with Scientists and Sages: The Search for Unity* (New York: Routledge & Kegan Paul, 1987), 182–190.

44–45   **A more fundamental transformation**: Susanne R. Cook-Greuter, "Making the Case for a Developmental Perspective," *Industrial and Commercial Training* 36, no. 7 (December 2004): 275–281, DOI: 10.1108/00197850410563902. This also parallels what's known as vertical development versus horizontal/lateral development.

47   **"dependable strengths"**: Dependable Strengths is now a registered trademark owned by the Center for Dependable Strengths (CDS).

47   **Peter Drucker described Haldane**: Bernard Haldane, *Career Satisfaction and Success: How to Know and Manage Your Strengths,* rev. ed., foreword by Peter Drucker (New York: AMACOM, 1988).

47   **Haldane's work**: Tan Vinh, "Bernard Haldane Was Career-Counseling Pioneer," *The Seattle Times*, July 27, 2002, accessed online February 26, 2021, https://archive.seattletimes.com/archive/?date=20020727&slug=haldane27m; "Bernard Haldane, 91, an Author and Innovator in Job Counseling," *The New York Times*, August 5, 2002, accessed online February 26, 2021, https://www.nytimes.com/2002/08/05/us/bernard-haldane-91-an-author-and-innovator-in-job-counseling.html; "The Center for Dependable Strengths Origins

& History," www.dependablestrengths.org/history. Bernard Haldane started his own company under his name in 1947 and sold it in the 1970s. He continued his work with the Dependable Strengths Project at the University of Washington in Seattle. It later became the Center for Dependable Strengths.

48   **Studies have shown that focusing**: Susan Sorenson, "How Employee Strengths Make Your Company Stronger," Gallup Business Journal, February 20, 2014, accessed online February 26, 2021, https://news.gallup.com/businessjournal/167462/employees-strengths-company-stronger.aspx; Jim Asplund, "When Americans Use Their Strengths More, They Stress Less," Gallup, September 27, 2012, accessed online December 12, 2021, https://news.gallup.com/poll/157679/americans-strengths-stress-less.aspx; Alex M. Wood et al., "Using Personal and Psychological Strengths Leads to Increases in Well-Being over Time: A Longitudinal Study and the Development of the Strengths Use Questionnaire," *Personality and Individual Differences* 50, no. 1 (January 2011): 15–19, DOI: 10.1016/j.paid.2010.08.004.

48   **A core strength, then, is**: My perspective on strengths has been influenced by Gallup's research on strengths (www.gallup.com/cliftonstrengths), Bernard Haldane's work, and the training I completed through the Center for Dependable Strengths (www.dependablestrengths.org).

48–49   **Mihaly Csikszentmihalyi called "flow"**: Csikszentmihalyi, *Flow*, 71–93; Martin E. P. Seligman, *Authentic Happiness: Using the New Positive Psychology to Realize Your*

Potential for Lasting Fulfillment (New York: Atria, 2013), 173–176.

51   **"No matter where I am . . ."**: John Kroger, interview with author, September 28, 2020.

51   **A meta-analysis of these studies**: Geoffrey L. Cohen and David K. Sherman, "The Psychology of Change: Self-Affirmation and Social Psychological Intervention," *Annual Review of Psychology* 65, no. 1 (January 2014): 333–371, DOI: 10.1146/annurev-psych-010213-115137.

52   **Other studies show**: Carnegie Mellon University, "Self-Affirmation Improves Problem-Solving Under Stress," ScienceDaily, accessed online September 23, 2020, https://www.sciencedaily.com/releases/2013/05/130503132956.htm; J. David Creswell et al., "Affirmation of Personal Values Buffers Neuroendocrine and Psychological Stress Responses," *Psychological Science* 16, no. 11 (November 2005): 846–851, DOI: 10.1111/j.1467-9280.2005.01624.x/.

53   **Lucy Helm underscored this**: Lucy Helm, interview with author, March 29, 2021.

53   **Konstantinos, also known as Kosta**: "'O Allos Anthropos' (Fellow Man)," Athens Living, YouTube, December 3, 2014, 3:43, accessed online November 2, 2020, https://www.youtube.com/watch?v=g57qnche3fM;   Annia Ciezadlo, "This Kid Came Up to Ask How Much the Food Cost. I Told Him It Was Free," September 10, 2015, Upworthy, https://www.upworthy.com/this-kid-came-up-to-ask-how-much-the-food-cost-i-told-him-it-was-free; Elyse Wanshel, "Greek Man Who Lost Job Now Works Full Time Feeding Those in Need," Huffington Post,

May 10, 2016, https://www.huffpost.com/entry/konstantinos-polychronopoulos-o-allos-anthropos-athens-greece-syrian-refugees_n_5730b4b5e4b0bc9cb04 76c80/.

55   **"We *make* our purpose"**: Carl Sagan, ed. Ann Druyen, *The Varieties of Scientific Experience: A Personal View of the Search for God* (New York: Penguin Books, 2007), 227. Emphasis his.

55   **Research has shown that having a purpose**: Stacey M. Schaefer et al., "Purpose in Life Predicts Better Emotional Recovery from Negative Stimuli," *PLoS ONE* 8, no. 11 (November 2013): e80329, DOI: 10.1371/journal.pone.0080329; Toshimasa Sone et al., "Sense of Life Worth Living (Ikigai) and Mortality in Japan: Ohsaki Study," *Psychosomatic Medicine* 70, no. 6 (July 2008): 709–715, DOI: 10.1097/PSY.0b013e31817e7e64; Steven E. Southwick and Dennis S. Charney, *Resilience: The Science of Mastering Life's Greatest Challenges* (Cambridge: Cambridge University Press, 2018), 251–267; Marta Zaraska, "Boosting Our Sense of Meaning in Life Is an Often Overlooked Longevity Ingredient," *The Washington Post*, January 3, 2021, accessed online November 23, 2021, https://www.washingtonpost.com/health/boosting-our-sense-of-meaning-in-life-is-an-often-overlooked-longevity-ingredient/2020/12/31/84871d32-29d4-11eb-8fa2-06e7cbb145c0_story.html; Emily Esfahani Smith, *The Power of Meaning: Crafting a Life that Matters* (New York: Crown, 2017), 14–15 and 93–95.

55 **people who felt they had a purpose**: Naina Dhingra et al., "Igniting Individual Purpose in Times of Crisis," *McKinsey Quarterly,* August 18, 2020, accessed online November 23, 2021, https://www.mckinsey.com/business-functions/people-and-organizational-performance/our-insights/igniting-individual-purpose-in-times-of-crisis/.

55–56 **the following parable shows**: Peter F. Drucker, *The Practice of Management* (New York: Harper and Brothers Publishers, 1954), 122; Bruce N. Pfau, "How an Accounting Firm Convinced its Employees They Could Change the World," *Harvard Business Review*, October 6, 2015, accessed online January 9, 2021, https://hbr.org/2015/10/how-an-accounting-firm-convinced-its-employees-they-could-change-the-world. There are many variations of this parable; mine is an adaptation and blend of how it is told in these sources.

56 **People who are job crafters**: Shankar Vedantam, "Finding Meaning at Work: How We Shape and Think about our Jobs," September 12, 2019, in *Hidden Brain*, podcast, accessed online January 9, 2021, https://www.npr.org/2019/09/12/760255265/finding-meaning-at-work-how-we-shape-and-think-about-our-jobs/.

56 **In a study Wrzesniewski and Dutton did**: Amy Wrzesniewski and Jane E. Dutton, "Crafting a Job: Revisioning Employees as Active Crafters of their Work," *The Academy of Management Review* 26, no. 2 (April 2001): 179–201, DOI: 10.5465/amr.2001.4378011.

57 **she knew *why* she did it**: Simon Sinek, *Start with Why:*

How Great Leaders Inspire Everyone to Take Action (New York: Portfolio/Penguin, 2011).

58   **"Throughout my career . . ."**: Lauren, interview with author, November 12, 2021.

60   **"Developing a purpose statement . . ."**: Emails to author, January 2023; phone call to author January 16, 2023.

60   **"use psychological science to help kids thrive"**: Angela Duckworth, *Grit: The Power of Passion and Perseverance* (New York: Scribner, 2016), 159.

60   **Crafting that statement**: Duckworth, *Grit*, 74.

CHAPTER 4

63   **"As my context changes . . ."**: Joe Fassler, "Amy Tan's Lonely, 'Pixel-by-Pixel' Writing Method," *The Atlantic*, December 10, 2013, accessed online May 4, 2021, https://www.theatlantic.com/entertainment/archive/2013/12/amy-tans-lonely-pixel-by-pixel-writing-method/282215/.

63   **In a study published in 2014**: David Robinson, "Psychologists Are Uncovering the Surprising Influence of Geography on Our Reasoning, Behaviour, and Sense of Self," BBC Future, January 19, 2017, accessed online April 8, 2021, https://www.bbc.com/future/article/20170118-how-east-and-west-think-in-profoundly-different-ways; T. Talhelm et al., "Large-Scale Psychological Differences Within China Explained by Rice Versus Wheat Culture," *Science* 344, no. 6184 (May 2014): 603–608, DOI: 10.1126/science.1246850/.

64   **every person carries their own mental frames**: Kendra
Cherry, "The Role of a Schema in Psychology," Verywell Mind, September 23, 2019, accessed online May
12, 2022, https://www.verywellmind.com/what-is-a-
schema-2795873; Lera Boroditsky, "How Language Shapes
Thought: The Languages We Speak Affect Our Perspectives of the World," *Scientific American*, February 2011,
63–65, https://www.scientificamerican.com/article/how-
language-shapes-thought/; Daniel J. Siegel, *Mindsight: The
New Science of Personal Transformation* (New York: Bantam
Books, 2011), 73; Lisa Feldman Barrett, *How Emotions Are
Made: The Secret Life of the Brain* (Boston: Mariner Books,
2018), 28–30.

64   **without our awareness**: Daniel Kahneman, *Thinking, Fast
and Slow* (New York: Farrar, Straus and Giroux, 2013),
20–30. This is related to what Nobel laureate and psychologist Daniel Kahneman describes as "fast thinking."

65   **Every second, the human brain processes**: David DiS-
alvo, "Your Brain Sees Even When You Don't," *Forbes*,
June 22, 2013, accessed online October 20, 2022, https://
www.forbes.com/sites/daviddisalvo/2013/06/22/your-
brain-sees-even-when-you-dont/?sh=4bd10a27116a; John
Coates, *The Hour Between Dog and Wolf: Risk Taking, Gut
Feelings and the Biology of Boom and Bust* (New York: The
Penguin Press, 2012), 74.

65   **the brain keeps out of our consciousness**: David
Eagleman, *The Brain: The Story of You* (New York: Vintage
Books, 2017), 61–62; Steve Ayan, "The Brain's Autopilot

Mechanism Steers Consciousness," *Scientific American*, December 19, 2018, accessed online May 6, 2021, https://www.scientificamerican.com/article/the-brains-autopilot-mechanism-steers-consciousness/; Charles Duhigg, *The Power of Habit: Why We Do What We Do in Life and Business* (New York: Random House Trade Paperbacks, 2014), 17–19.

65   **much like water is to fish**: David Foster Wallace, "This Is Water," Kenyon College Commencement Speech, May 21, 2005, https://fs.blog/david-foster-wallace-this-is-water/.

66   **we instinctively dislike uncertainty**: David Rock, "A Hunger for Certainty: Your Brain Craves Certainty and Avoids Uncertainty Like It's Pain," *Psychology Today*, October 25, 2009, accessed online July 21, 2021, https://www.psychologytoday.com/us/blog/your-brain-work/200910/hunger-certainty/.

67   **participants preferred to know *for certain***: Archy O. de Berker et al., "Computations of Uncertainty Mediate Acute Stress Responses in Humans," *Nature Communications* 7 (March 2016): 10996, DOI: 10.1038/ncomms10996; Yvette Brazier, "Uncertainty Is More Stressful Than Pain, Say Neurologists," Medical News Today, March 30, 2016, accessed online April 4, 2022, https://www.medicalnewstoday.com/articles/308418; Barrett, *How Emotions Are Made*, 213.

67   **Uncertainty *helps* us be creative**: Ephrat Livni, "A New Study from Yale Scientists Shows How Uncertainty Helps Us Learn," Quartz, July 31, 2018, accessed online August

29, 2021, https://qz.com/1343503/a-new-study-from-yale-scientists-shows-how-uncertainty-helps-us-learn/; KC Ifeanyi and Dr. Ron Beghetto, "How Uncertainty Can Make Us More Creative," September 26, 2019, in *Creative Control*, podcast, 22:43, https://podcasts.apple.com/us/podcast/how-uncertainty-can-make-us-more-creative/id1393035409?i=1000451296133/.

67   **influence our reasoning, emotions, and actions**: George Lakoff and Mark Johnson, *Metaphors We Live By* (Chicago: The University of Chicago Press, 1980; with a new afterword, 2003), 145 and 245–251; Richard, Nordquist, "Understanding Conceptual Metaphors," ThoughtCo., accessed online May 15, 2020, https://www.thoughtco.com/what-is-conceptual-metaphor-1689899/.

67   **they can be confusing**: James Geary, *I Is an Other: The Secret Life of Metaphor and How It Shapes the Way We See the World* (New York: Harper Perennial, 2012), 44–52; Kinga Morsanyia, Dušan Stamenković, and Keith J. Holyoak, "Metaphor Processing in Autism: A Systemic Review and Meta-Analysis," *Developmental Review* 57 (2020): 100925, DOI: 10.1016/j.dr.2020.100925.

68   **One study published in 2011**: Paul H. Thibodeau and Lera Boroditsky, "Metaphors We Think With: The Role of Metaphor in Reasoning," *PLoS ONE* 6, no. 2 (February 2011): e16782, DOI: 10.1371/journal.pone.0016782/.

68   **"Many times in our research . . ."**: Szu-chi Huang, interview with author, June 10, 2021. All quotes from Dr. Huang are from that interview.

69   **To find out, they conducted six studies**: Szu-Chi Huang and Jennifer Aaker, "It's the Journey, Not the Destination: How Metaphor Drives Growth after Goal Attainment," *Journal of Personality and Social Psychology: Attitudes and Social Cognition* 117, no. 4 (June 2019): 697–720, DOI: 10.1037/pspa0000164/.

70   **Metaphors help us grapple with ideas**: George Lakoff, "Mapping the Brain's Metaphor Circuitry: Metaphorical Thought in Everyday Reason," *Frontiers in Human Neuroscience* 8 (December 2014): 958, DOI: 10.3389/fnhum.2014.00958; Geary, *I Is an Other*, 169; Anja Jamrozik et al., "Metaphor: Bridging Embodiment to Abstraction," *Psychonomic Bulletin & Review* 23, no. 4 (August 2016): 1080–1089, DOI: 10.3758/s13423-015-0861-0/.

71   **your brain actually *maps* it**: Lakoff and Johnson, *Metaphors We Live By*, 257–258; Lakoff, "Mapping the Brain's Metaphor Circuitry"; Geary, *I Is an Other*, 94–111; Michael Chorost, "Your Brain on Metaphors," *The Chronicle of Higher Education*, September 1, 2014, accessed online April 11, 2021, https://www.chronicle.com/article/Your-Brain-on -Metaphors/148495; Huang and Aaker, "It's the Journey, Not the Destination," 699; Jamrozik et al., "Metaphor: Bridging Embodiment to Abstraction"; Mathias Benedek et al., "Creating Metaphors: The Neural Basis of Figurative Language Production," *NeuroImage* 90 (April 2014): 99–106, DOI: 10.1016/j.neuroimage.2013.12.046/.

71   **"I am having a rough day"**: Quinn Eastman, "Say It with Feeling: Metaphors Activate Sensory Part of Brain,"

Emory University News Center, February 8, 2012, http://news.emory.edu/stories/2012/02/metaphor_brain_imaging/campus.html; Simon Lacey, Randall Stilla, and K. Sathian, "Metaphorically Feeling: Comprehending Textural Metaphors Activates Somatosensory Cortex," *Brain and Language* 120, no. 3 (March 2012): 416–421, DOI: 10.1016/j.bandl.2011.12.016/. Dr. Sathian's research used sentences with textural metaphors, which activated the parietal operculum (a brain region key for sensing texture through touch).

71   **"standing on a balcony"**: Ronald Heifetz, Alexander Grashow, and Marty Linksy, *The Practice of Adaptive Leadership: Tools and Tactics for Changing Your Organization and the World* (Boston: Harvard Business Press, 2009), 7–8.

73   **"Battling" cancer suggests that patients "lose"**: Ian Sample, "'War on Cancer' Metaphors May Do Harm, Research Shows," *The Guardian*, August 10, 2019, accessed online April 11, 2021, https://www.theguardian.com/society/2019/aug/10/war-cancer-metaphors-harm-research-shows/.

73   **When an argument is framed as a "war"**: Lakoff and Johnson, *Metaphors We Live By*, 4–5.

73   **"New metaphors have the power . . ."**: Lakoff and Johnson, *Metaphors We Live By*, 145.

73   **it's more like a painting**: Daniel Gilbert, *Stumbling on Happiness* (New York: Vintage Books, 2007), 94.

74   **Because of the negativity bias**: Kendra Cherry, "What Is the Negativity Bias?," Verywell Mind, September 14, 2022, accessed online November 7, 2022, https://www.

verywellmind.com/negative-bias-4589618; David Rock, *Your Brain at Work: Strategies for Overcoming Distraction, Regaining Focus, and Working Smarter All Day Long* (New York: Harper Business, 2009), 109–110.

74   **While problems should not be ignored**: See also: David L. Cooperrider and Diana Whitney, *Appreciative Inquiry: A Positive Revolution in Change* (San Francisco: Berrett-Koehler, 2005).

74   **addressing child malnutrition in Vietnamese villages**: David Dorsey, "Positive Deviant," *Fast Company*, November 30, 2000, accessed online May 18, 2021, https://www. fastcompany.com/42075/positive-deviant; Chip Heath and Dan Heath, *Switch: How to Change Things When Change Is Hard* (New York: Broadway Books, 2010), 27–32.

75   **health and well-being improve**: Madhuleena Roy Chowdhury, "The Neuroscience of Gratitude and How It Affects Anxiety and Grief," PositivePsychology.com, October 9, 2021, accessed online October 10, 2021, https:// positivepsychology.com/neuroscience-of-gratitude/.

76   **this story is not confirmed**: Bill Casselman, "The Legend of Abraham Wald," American Mathematical Society, June 2016, accessed online May 16, 2022, https://www.ams. org/publicoutreach/feature-column/fc-2016-06/.

76   **preparing them to tackle a challenge**: Jeremy P. Jamieson et al., "Turning the Knots in Your Stomach into Bows: Reappraising Arousal Improves Performance on the GRE," *Journal of Experimental Social Psychology* 46, no. 1 (January 2010): 208–212, DOI: 10.1016/j.jesp.2009.08.015; Kelly

McGonigal, *The Upside of Stress: Why Stress Is Good for You, and How to Get Good at It* (New York: Avery, 2016), 8–10; "Reframing Stress Could Help People Overcome Public Speaking Phobia, Study Suggests," Huffington Post, April 21, 2013, accessed online May 31, 2022, https://www.huffpost.com/entry/reframing-stress-public-speaking-phobia-stage-fright_n_3055664/.

77   **shift your attention to the meaning behind it**: Shawn Achor, *Big Potential: Five Secrets of Reaching Higher by Powering Those around You* (London: Virgin Books, 2018), 164–166.

77   **Created by business writer**: Suzy Welch, "The Rule of 10-10-10," *O, The Oprah Magazine*, September 2006, accessed online November 8, 2022, https://www.oprah.com/spirit/suzy-welchs-rule-of-10-10-10-decision-making-guide/all/.

78   **people *who are like us***: Carsten K. W. De Dreu et al., "Oxytocin Modulates Selection of Allies in Intergroup Conflict," *Proceedings of the Royal Society B* 279, no. 1731 (March 2012): 1150–1154, DOI: 10.1098/rspb.2011.1444; Robert M. Sapolsky, *Behave: The Biology of Humans at Our Best and Worst* (New York: Penguin Books, 2018), 388–424.

79   **the pharmaceutical company Eli Lilly**: David Epstein, *Range: Why Generalists Triumph in a Specialized World* (New York: Riverhead Books, 2019), 171–173.

80   **"Big innovation most often happens . . ."**: Epstein, *Range*, 178.

80   **can also spark creative ideas**: Katherine W. Phillips, "How Diversity Makes Us Smarter," *Scientific American*, October 1, 2014, https://www.scientificamerican.com/article/how-diversity-makes-us-smarter/.

81   **takes intention and mental energy**: Rock, *Your Brain at Work*, 133; Sapolsky, *Behave*, 60–61.

CHAPTER 5

83   **"Whether you are overwhelmed . . ."**: Kelly McGonigal, *The Upside of Stress: Why Stress is Good for You and How to Get Good at It* (New York: Avery, 2015), 140.

83   **Campbell describes this timeless trek**: Joseph Campbell, *The Hero with a Thousand Faces*, 3rd ed. (Novato: New World Library, 2008), 41–48 and 64–79.

83   **It's one of the most common narrative arcs**: Will Linn, "Joseph Campbell Is the Hidden Link between '2001,' 'Star Wars,' and 'Mad Max: Fury Road,'" IndieWire, March 12, 2018, accessed online August 13, 2021, https://www.indiewire.com/2018/03/joseph-campbell-heros-journey-2001-star-wars-1201937470/.

84   **"the familiar life horizon . . ."**: Campbell, *The Hero with a Thousand Faces*, 43.

84   **we're more likely to explore**: Inge Bretherton, "The Origins of Attachment Theory: John Bowlby and Mary Ainsworth," *Developmental Psychology* 28, no. 5 (September 1992): 759–775, DOI: 10.1037/0012-1649.28.5.759; Herminia Ibarra, *Working Identity: Unconventional Strategies for Reinventing Your Career* (Boston: Harvard Business

School Press, 2004), 130–132; Marcia B. Baxter Magolda, *Authoring Your Life: Developing Your Internal Voice to Navigate Life's Challenges* (Sterling: Stylus Publishing, 2009), 249–279.

85   **the 1988 PBS documentary**: *Joseph Campbell and the Power of Myth*, 25th Anniversary Edition, 2012, Athena/PBS, 05:44:00, https://billmoyers.com/series/joseph-campbell-and-the-power-of-myth-1988/.

86   **Their relief is palpable**: Ethan Kross, *Chatter: The Voice in Our Head, Why It Matters, and How to Harness It* (New York: Crown, 2021), 82–85. "Normalizing" or "normalization" happens when we realize we're not alone in an experience, which is comforting.

86   **One of them told me later**: 2016–17 leadership program participant, interview with author, November 20, 2020.

86   **that need for belonging runs deep**: Roy F. Baumeister and Mark R. Leary, "The Need to Belong: Desire for Interpersonal Attachments as a Fundamental Human Motivation," *Psychological Bulletin* 117, no. 3 (May 1995): 497–529, DOI: 10.1037/0033-2909.117.3.497/.

86   **the same areas of the brain are activated**: Ethan Kross et al., "Social Rejection Shares Somatosensory Representations with Physical Pain," *Proceedings of the National Academy of Sciences of the United States of America* 108, no. 15 (March 2011): 6270–6275, DOI: 10.1073/pnas.1102693108; Naomi I. Eisenberger, Matthew D. Lieberman, and Kipling D. Williams, "Does Rejection Hurt? An fMRI Study of Social Exclusion," *Science* 302, no. 5643 (October 2003):

290–292, DOI: 10.1126/science.1089134; Geoff Mac-Donald and Mark R. Leary, "Why Does Social Exclusion Hurt? The Relationship between Social and Physical Pain," *Psychological Bulletin* 131, no. 2 (March 2005): 202–223, DOI: 10.1037/0033-2909.131.2.202/.

86   **Feeling disconnected**: John T. Cacioppo and William Patrick, *Loneliness: Human Nature and the Need for Social Connection* (New York: W.W. Norton & Company, 2008), 29–41 and 103.

87   **helps regulate our nervous systems**: Fatih Ozbay et al., "Social Support and Resilience to Stress: From Neurobiology to Clinical Practice," *Psychiatry* (Edgmont) 4, no. 5 (May 2007): 35–40, https://www.ncbi.nlm.nih.gov/pmc/articles/PMC2921311/; McGonigal, *The Upside of Stress*, 135–42; Bessel Van Der Kolk, *The Body Keeps the Score: Brain, Mind, and Body in the Healing of Trauma* (New York: Viking, 2014), 79; Jane E. Brody, "Social Interaction Is Critical for Mental and Emotional Health," *The New York Times*, June 12, 2017, accessed online September 8, 2021, https://www.nytimes.com/2017/06/12/well/live/having-friends-is-good-for-you.html; Cacioppo and Patrick, *Loneliness*, 37; Lisa Feldman Barrett, *How Emotions Are Made: The Secret Life of the Brain* (New York: Mariner Books, 2018), 196–197.

88   **This pair of studies**: Simone Schnall et al., "Social Support and the Perception of Geographical Slant," *Journal of Experimental Social Psychology* 44, no. 5 (September 2008): 1246–1255, DOI: 10.1016/j.jesp.2008.04.011/.

89   **As several studies have shown**: Howard S. Friedman and Ronald E. Riggio, "Effect of Individual Differences in Nonverbal Expressiveness on Transmission of Emotion," *Journal of Nonverbal Behavior* 6, no. 2 (January 1981): 96–104, DOI: 10.1007/BF00987285; Elaine Hatfield et al., "New Perspectives on Emotional Contagion: A Review of Classic and Recent Research on Facial Mimicry and Contagion," *Interpersona: An International Journal on Personal Relationships* 8, no. 2 (December 2014): 159–179, DOI: 10.5964/ijpr.v8i2.162; Sigal Barsade, "The Contagion We Can Control," *Harvard Business Review*, March 26, 2020, accessed online September 8, 2021, https://hbr.org/2020/03/the-contagion-we-can-control; Sigal G. Barsade, Constantinos G.V. Coutifaris, and Julianna Pillemer, "Emotional Contagion in Organizational Life," *Research in Organizational Behavior* 38 (December 2018): 137–151, DOI: 10.1016/j.riob.2018.11.005/; Shawn Achor, *Big Potential: Five Secrets of Reaching Higher by Powering Those Around You* (London: Virgin Books, 2018), 40–41.

90   **studies have also shown**: J. Holt-Lunstad, "Loneliness and Social Isolation as Risk Factors: The Power of Social Connection in Prevention," *American Journal of Lifestyle Medicine* 15, no. 5 (May 2021): 567–573, DOI: 10.1177/15598276211009454; Steven M. Southwick and Dennis S. Charney, *Resilience: The Science of Mastering Life's Greatest Challenges*, 2nd ed. (Cambridge: Cambridge University Press, 2018), 148–153; Gabriella Rosen Kellerman and Martin Seligman, *Tomorrowmind: Thriving at*

Work with Resilience, Creativity, and Connection—Now and in an Uncertain Future (New York: Atria Books, 2023), 107–118; Baxter Magolda, *Authoring Your Life*.

90   **In one longitudinal study**: Baxter Magolda, *Authoring Your Life*.

91   **"It started with basic training . . ."**: Ray, interview with author, August 7, 2020.

92   **"That really helped me a lot . . ."**: Patti Occhiuzzo Giggans, interview with author, July 14, 2022.

95   ***helping others feels good***: McGonigal, *The Upside of Stress*, 138–141; Adam Grant, *Give and Take: A Revolutionary Approach to Success* (New York: Viking, 2013), 166–168; Elizabeth Bernstein, "Why Being Kind Helps You, Too—Especially Now," *The Wall Street Journal*, August 11, 2020, accessed online September 16, 2021, https://www.wsj.com/articles/why-being-kind-helps-you-tooespecially-now-11597194000; Eva Ritvo, "The Neuroscience of Giving," *Psychology Today*, April 24, 2014, accessed online September 16, 2021, https://www.psychologytoday.com/us/blog/vitality/201404/the-neuroscience-giving/.

95   **"When you help someone else . . ."**: McGonigal, *The Upside of Stress*, 156 and 155.

96   **She cites several studies**: McGonigal, *The Upside of Stress*, 156–157.

96   **Researchers from several top universities**: McGonigal, *The Upside of Stress*, 141–142; Cassie Mogilner, Zoë Chance, and Michael I. Norton, "Giving Time Gives You Time," *Association for Psychological Science* 23, no. 10 (September 2012): 1233–1238, DOI: 10.1177/0956797612442551/.

98   **trauma expert Laura van Dernoot Lipsky**: Laura van Dernoot Lipsky, *The Age of Overwhelm: Strategies for the Long Haul* (Oakland: Berrett-Koehler Publishers, 2018), 4.

98   **"co-rumination"**: Kross, *Chatter*, 93.

98–99 **Psychologist Ethan Kross recommends**: Kross, *Chatter*, 93–101.

CHAPTER 6

101   **"I wondered . . ."**: Mae Jemison, "Teach Arts and Sciences Together," TED Talk, February 2002, 21:09, accessed online November 9, 2021, https://www.ted.com/talks/mae_jemison_teach_arts_and_sciences_together.

101   **Maya Shankar loved playing the violin**. Maya Shankar, interview with author, April 2, 2016; Maya Shankar, email messages to author, June 2021. All quotes are from these exchanges unless otherwise noted.

102   **"When you're thinking about next steps . . ."**: "Google's Maya Shankar Delivers Keynote at Velocity 2019, UCLA Anderson's Women's Summit," UCLA Anderson, YouTube, 31:37, February 20, 2019, accessed online June 30, 2021, https://www.youtube.com/watch?v=h9ytufBRw4o/.

103   **I hadn't realized how many types**: George Loewenstein, "The Psychology of Curiosity: A Review and Reinterpretation," *Psychological Bulletin* 116, no. 1 (July 1994): 75–98, DOI: 10.1037/0033-2909.116.1.75; Todd B. Kashdan, Paul Rose, and Frank D. Fincham, "Curiosity and Exploration: Facilitating Positive Subjective Experiences and

Personal Growth Opportunities," *Journal of Personality Assessment* 82, no. 3 (July 2004): 291–305, DOI: 10.1207/s15327752jpa8203_05; Jordan A. Litman and Paul J. Silvia, "The Latent Structure of Trait Curiosity: Evidence for Interest and Deprivation Curiosity Dimensions," *Journal of Personality Assessment* 86, no. 3 (June 2006): 318–328, DOI: 10.1207/s15327752jpa8603_07; Todd B. Kashdan et al., "The Five Dimensions of Curiosity," *Harvard Business Review Magazine*, September–October 2018, accessed online December 20, 2022, https://hbr.org/2018/09/the-five-dimensions-of-curiosity; Mario Livio, *Why?: What Makes Us Curious* (New York: Simon & Schuster, 2017).

104   **Dr. Judson Brewer**: Judson Brewer, "The Science of Curiosity," Mindful, January 6, 2022, accessed online December 20, 2022, https://www.mindful.org/the-science-of-curiosity/. Dr. Brewer is describing the difference between deprivation curiosity (D-curiosity) and interest curiosity (I-curiosity) identified by psychologists Jordan Litman and Paul Silvia.

104   **As Dr. Brewer explains it**: Brewer, "The Science of Curiosity."

104   **"Most people stop looking . . ."**: Todd Kashdan, *Curious?: Discover the Missing Ingredient to a Fulfilling Life* (New York: Harper, 2010), 17.

105   **research suggests that curiosity peaks**: Francesca Gino, *Rebel Talent: Why It Pays to Break the Rules at Work and in Life* (New York: Dey Street, 2018), 49; Monica C. Parker, *The Power of Wonder: The Extraordinary Emotion That Will*

Change the Way You Live, Learn, and Lead (New York: TarcherPerigee, 2023), 104; Livio, *Why?*, 94. However, other research suggests that specific and epistemic curiosity can stay constant throughout our lives.

105   **And when people aren't curious**: Ian Leslie, *Curious: The Desire to Know and Why Your Future Depends on It* (New York: Basic Books, 2014), 31.

107   **Shifting from the constrictive framing of "should"**: Gino, *Rebel Talent*, 84–85.

108   **Sully wrote in his memoir**: Chesley B. "Sully" Sullenberger III and Jeffrey Zaslow, *Sully: The Untold Story behind the Miracle of the Hudson* (New York: William Morrow, 2016), 211.

108   **"I knew I had to solve this problem . . ."**: "I Was Sure I Could Do It," *60 Minutes*, CBS, YouTube, 11:19, https://www.youtube.com/watch?v=rZ5HnyEQg7M/.

109   **Sully credits his ability**: "I Was Sure I Could Do It," *60 Minutes*; Francesca Gino, "The Business Case for Curiosity," *Harvard Business Review Magazine*, September–October 2018, accessed online November 18, 2021, https://hbr.org/2018/09/the-business-case-for-curiosity/.

110   **There's "wondering about"**: Robert Kegan, *In Over Our Heads: The Mental Demands of Modern Life* (Cambridge: Harvard University Press, 1994), 8.

110   **each one is a sun**: Catherine Zuckerman, "Everything You Wanted to Know about Stars," *National Geographic*, March 20, 2019, accessed online December 18, 2022, https://www.nationalgeographic.com/science/article/stars

110   **wonder expands curiosity**: Marina Bazhydai and Gert Westermann, "From Curiosity, to Wonder, to Creativity: A Cognitive Psychology Perspective," in ed. Anders Schinkel *Wonder, Education, and Human Flourishing* (Amsterdam: VU University Press, 2020); Alice Chirico et al., "Awe Enhances Creative Thinking: An Experimental Study," *Creativity Research Journal* 30, no. 2 (April 2018): 123–31, DOI: 10.1080/10400419.2018.1446491.

110   **The two work together in a virtuous cycle**: Parker, *The Power of Wonder*, 94.

110   **a dramatic effect on our bodies**: Dacher Keltner, *Awe: The New Science of Everyday Wonder and How It Can Transform Your Life* (New York: Penguin Press, 2023), 249; Hope Reese, "How a Bit of Awe Can Improve Your Health," *The New York Times*, January 3, 2023, accessed online June 11, 2023, https://www.nytimes.com/2023/01/03/well/live/awe-wonder-dacher-keltner.html; Jennifer Stellar et al., "Positive Affect and Markers of Discrete Positive Emotions Predict Lower Levels of Inflammatory Cytokines," *Emotion* 15, no. 2 (April 2015): 129–133, DOI: 10.1037/emo0000033/.

110–111   **a much bigger, interconnected world**: Keltner, *Awe*, 34–40; Michelle N. Shiota, Dacher Keltner, and Amanda Mossman, "The Nature of Awe: Elicitors, Appraisals, and Effects on Self-Concept," *Cognition and Emotion* 21, no. 5 (August 2007): 944–963, DOI: 10.1080/02699930600923668/.

111   **"Wonder defamiliarizes the familiar . . ."**: Anders Schinkel,

"The Educational Importance of Deep Wonder," *Journal of Philosophy of Education* 51, no. 2 (February 2017): 543, DOI: 10.1111/1467-9752.12233.

111   **"I remember being so delighted . . ."**: Jeanette, interviews with author, March 6, 2020, and January 2, 2023.

112   **"our brain tries to make sense . . ."**: Parker, *The Power of Wonder*, 81.

113   **Rachel Carson used to ask herself**: Parker, *The Power of Wonder*, 216.

114   **they were using navigating expertise**: Felipe Fernández-Armesto, *Pathfinders: A Global History of Exploration* (New York: W.W. Norton & Company, 2007),43–50; David Lewis, *We, the Navigators: The Ancient Art of Landfinding in the Pacific* (Honolulu: The University Press of Hawaii, 1975), 11 and 277–292; ed. K.R. Howe, *Vaka Moana Voyages of the Ancestors: The Discovery and Settlement of the Pacific* (Honolulu: University of Hawaii Press, 2007), 79 and 156–197.

114   **a seahorse-shaped structure in the brain**: "Hippocampus," Britannica.com, accessed online January 23, 2021, https://www.britannica.com/science/hippocampus; Tula Karras, *Memory: What It Is, How It Works, and Ways You Can Improve It*, Single Issue Magazine, *National Geographic*, November 13, 2020, 23–25; M.R. O'Connor, *Wayfinding: The Science and Mystery of How Humans Navigate the World* (New York: St. Martin's Press, 2019), 6–9. There are actually two hippocampi, one on each side of the brain, in the medial temporal lobe. It's commonly described as shaped like a seahorse (thus

therefore its name, from the Greek *hippos*, "horse," and *kampos*, "sea monster").

114   **along with other parts of the brain**: Karras, *Memory*; David Eagleman, *Livewired: The Inside Story of the Ever-Changing Brain* (New York: Pantheon Books, 2020), 207–231.

114   **creating a mental map**: O'Connor, *Wayfinding*, 7 and 161–182.

114   **you try to anticipate each choice's outcome**: Kenneth Kay et al., "Constant Sub-Second Cycling between Representations of Possible Futures in the Hippocampus," *Cell* 180, no. 3 (February 2020): 552–567, E25, DOI: 10.1016/j.cell.2020.01.014/.

115   **like a librarian**: Jonathan Webb, "Peeking into the Brain's Filing System," BBC News, July 5, 2015, accessed online November 9, 2021, https://www.bbc.com/news/science-environment-33380677/.

115   **combines bits of memory into various**: David Eagleman, *The Brain: The Story of You* (New York: Vintage Books, 2017), 28; Donna Rose Addis and Daniel L. Schacter, "The Hippocampus and Future: Where Do We Stand?" *Frontiers in Human Neuroscience* 5 (January 2012): 173, DOI: 10.3389/fnhum.2011.00173; Sinéad L. Mullaly and Eleanor A. Maguire, "Memory, Imagination, and Predicting the Future," *Neuroscientist* 20, no. 3 (June 2014): 220–234, DOI: 10.1177/1073858413495091/.

115   **This is one of the superpowers**: Eagleman, *The Brain*, 124–128; O'Connor, *Wayfinding*, 61.

115   **Curiosity primes the hippocampus**: Matthias J. Gruber, Bernard D. Gelman, and Charan Ranganath, "States of Curiosity Modulate Hippocampus-Dependent Learning via the Dopaminergic Circuit," *Neuron* 84, no. 2 (October 2014): 486–496, DOI: 10.1016/j.neuron.2014.08.060; Daisy Yuhas, "Curiosity Prepares the Brain for Better Learning," *Scientific American*, October 2, 2014, https:// www.scientificamerican.com/article/curiosity-prepares-the -brain-for-better-learning/.

115   **staying curious about a broad range**: David Eagleman and Anthony Brandt, *The Runaway Species: How Human Creativity Remakes the World* (New York: Catapult, 2017), 38–54; David Epstein, *Range: Why Generalists Triumph in a Specialized World* (New York: Riverhead Books, 2019).

116   **Maya Shankar recommends**: Maya Shankar, interview with author, April 2, 2016.

116   **scenario planning**: J. Peter Scoblic, "Learning from the Future," *Harvard Business Review Magazine*, July–August 2020, accessed online November 22, 2021, https:// hbr.org/2020/07/learning-from-the-future; Emmanuel Lagarrigue and Rafael Ramirez, "If Only We Knew. With Scenario Planning, We Do. Here's How to Prepare Better for the Next Crisis," World Economic Forum, November 10, 2020, accessed online November 22, 2021; Paul Schoemaker "Scenario Planning," *The Palgrave Encyclopedia of Strategic Management*, June 2016, 1–9, DOI: 10.1057/978-1-349-94848-2_652-1/.

117   **"It isn't really about the specific scenarios . . ."**: Sarah Chesemore, interview with author, December 11, 2020.

117   **Imagine Five Futures**: Julia Cameron, *The Artist's Way: A Spiritual Path to Higher Creativity* (New York: Tarcher/Putnam, 1992), 39–40. The Five Futures exercise is inspired by Julia Cameron's Five Lives exercise in *The Artist's Way*.

119   **they named the rover**: "'Curiosity,' Meet Clara," NASA Science Mars Exploration, June 8, 2009, https://mars.nasa.gov/news/112/curiosity-meet-clara/; "Mars Curiosity Rover," NASA Science Mars Exploration, accessed online November 9, 2021, https://mars.nasa.gov/msl/home/. Sixth-grader Clara Ma won the rover naming contest in 2009.

CHAPTER 7

121   **"Improvisation is the courage to move . . ."**: While commonly attributed to Bobby McFerrin, the exact source is unknown.

122   **Research shows that people who have an inspiring vision**: Richard Boyatzis, Melvin Smith, and Ellen Van Oosten, *Helping People Change: Coaching with Compassion for Lifelong Learning and Growth* (Boston: Harvard Business Review Press, 2019); Angela Passarelli, "Vision-Based Coaching: Optimizing Resources for Leader Development," *Frontiers in Psychology* 6 (April 2015): 412, DOI: 10.3389/fpsyg.2015.00412; Gabriella Rosen Kellerman and Martin Seligman, *Tomorrowmind: Thriving at Work with Resilience, Creativity, and Connection—Now and in an Uncertain Future* (New York: Atria Books, 2023), 70–71.

123   **research by Gabriele Oettingen**: Gabriele Oettingen,

Rethinking Positive Thinking: Inside the New Science of Motivation (New York: Portfolio, 2015). Oettingen notes caveats in her research, including that someone needed to believe their vision is possible for the "mental contrasting" of vision and barriers to result in motivated action.

124   **"We can only see so far . . ."**: adrienne maree brown, *Emergent Strategy: Shaping Change, Changing Worlds* (Chico: AK Press, 2017), 239.

124   **Manny Medina**: Manny Medina, interview with author, September 20, 2021.

125   **Ali Monguno, a Dubai-based architect**: Ali Monguno, interview with author, July 21, 2021.

126   **helps you bypass the fear reaction**: Robert Maurer, *One Small Step Can Change Your Life: The Kaizen Way* (New York: Workman Publishing, 2004), 26–27.

126   **As you complete each action**: Ralph Ryback, "The Science of Accomplishing Your Goals," *Psychology Today*, October 3, 2016, accessed online September 25, 2023, https://www.psychologytoday.com/us/blog/the-truisms-wellness/201610/the-science-accomplishing-your-goals/.

126   **"When I'm overwhelmed by a big goal . . ."**: Deeann, interview with author, October 25, 2023.

127   **"If you make a little bit of progress . . ."**: Manny Medina, interview with author, September 20, 2021.

128   **Take a break every ninety minutes**: "Research Proves Your Brain Needs Breaks," *Microsoft Work Trend Index Special Report*, April 20, 2021, accessed online July 10, 2023, https://www.microsoft.com/en-us/worklab/work-trend-index/brain-research/.

130   **psychologist and neuroscientist Ethan Kross**: Ethan Kross, *Chatter: The Voice in Our Head, Why It Matters, and How to Harness It* (New York: Crown, 2021), 71–77.

130   **"It's a lot easier for people to give advice . . ."**: Liz Greene, "How to Quiet Your Mind Chatter," *Nautilus*, March 10, 2021, accessed online October 7, 2021, https://nautil.us/issue/98/mind/how-to-quiet-your-mind-chatter/.

131   **"What brought me to the point of creativity . . ."**: Dirs. Jennifer Beamish and Toby Trackman, *The Creative Brain*, 2019, BlinkFilms, Netflix, 0:52:00, https://www.netflix.com/title/81090128.

131   **Khine remembered a favorite toy**: Dirs. Beamish and Trackman, *The Creative Brain*; "Toy Innovation in Tech Biochips," UCI News, September 9, 2009, accessed online October 11, 2021, https://news.uci.edu/2009/09/09/toy-inspires-innovation-in-high-tech-biochips/.

132   **your creative idea showed up**: Mark Jung-Beeman et al., "Neural Basis of Solving Problems with Insight," *PLoS Biology* 2, no. 4 (April 2004): e111, DOI: 10.1371/journal.pbio.0020111; Benjamin Baird et al., "Inspired by Distraction: Mind Wandering Facilitates Creative Incubation," *Psychological Science*, 23, no. 10, (2012), 117–22, DOI: 10.1177/0956797612446024.

133–134   **For example**: Matthew Walker, *Why We Sleep: Unlocking the Power of Sleep and Dreams* (New York: Scribner, 2018), 221 and 232.

134   **Sleep expert Matthew Walker says**: Walker, *Why We Sleep*, 132.

134   **can result in rumination**: Kieran C.R. Fox et al., "The Wandering Brain: Meta-Analysis of Functional Neuroimaging Studies of Mind-Wandering and Related Spontaneous Thought Processes," *NeuroImage* 111 (May 2015): 611–621, DOI: 10.1016/j.neuroimage.2015.02.039/.

135   **when it's hard and messy**: Frank Barrett, *Yes to the Mess: Surprising Leadership Lessons from Jazz* (Boston: Harvard Business Review Press, 2012).

135   **"I *cannot* lose this restaurant . . ."**: Bethany Jean Clement, "How a Seattle Chef Lost Her James Beard Award-Winning Restaurant but Came Out Hopeful after an Unreal Pandemic Year," *The Seattle Times*, March 13, 2021, accessed online October 15, 2021, https://www.seattletimes.com/life/food-drink/how-a-seattle-chef-lost-her-james-beard-award-winning-restaurant-but-came-out-hopeful-after-an-unreal-pandemic-year/.

135   **"It's our creativity . . ."**: Clement, "How a Seattle Chef."

136   **a cognitive bias called "sunk-cost fallacy"**: Daniel Kahneman, *Thinking, Fast and Slow* (New York: Farrar, Straus and Giroux, 2013), 345–346.

138   **increases our sense of agency**: David Rock, *Your Brain at Work: Strategies for Overcoming Distraction, Regaining Focus, and Working Smarter All Day Long* (New York: Harper Business, 2009), 123–126.

139   **research backs this up**: Steven M. Southwick and Dennis S. Charney, *Resilience: The Science of Mastering Life's Greatest Challenges*, 2nd ed. (Cambridge: Cambridge University Press, 2018), 261–263.

CONCLUSION

141   **"The future is uncertain. . . . But this . . ."**: Ilya Prigogine, ed. David Lorimer, "A (Very) Brief History of Certainty," *Scientific and Medical Network*, no. 56 (1995): 6–7.

143   **"One of the greatest lessons life has taught me . . ."**: Michelle Obama, *The Light We Carry: Overcoming in Uncertain Times* (New York: Crown, 2022), 248.

143   **"it helps if you're able to stay agile . . ."**: Obama, *The Light We Carry*, 277. Emphasis added.

144   **sustained his signature optimism**: Michael J. Fox, *No Time Like the Future: An Optimist Considers Mortality* (New York: Flatiron Books, 2020).

144   **"optimism is informed hope"**: Elisabeth Egan, "When It Comes to Living with Uncertainty, Michael J. Fox Is a Pro" *The New York Times*, November 13, 2020, accessed online February 19, 2021, https://www.nytimes.com/2020/11/13/books/michael-j-fox-no-time-like-the-future.html/.

INDEX

ABOUT THE AUTHOR

Jen Martin is a coach and consultant working with leaders and teams to navigate change creatively. For more than a decade, she has coached and trained thousands of people across industries and sectors, including Fortune 500 companies, start-ups, nonprofits, and government agencies. Jen began her career in public relations in Chicago working with large companies and transitioned to nonprofit and foundation leadership before launching her own consulting and coaching business. Jen has a B.A. in history and international studies from Northwestern University and an M.P.A. from the University of Washington with a focus on management and organization development. She is a certified professional coach, trained through CTI and certified through the International Coaching Federation. She currently lives in Seattle with her family and still has the love of adventure she gained from growing up in Alaska.

Learn more at jenmartinco.com. For downloadable book tools, please visit tools.thecreativewayforward.com

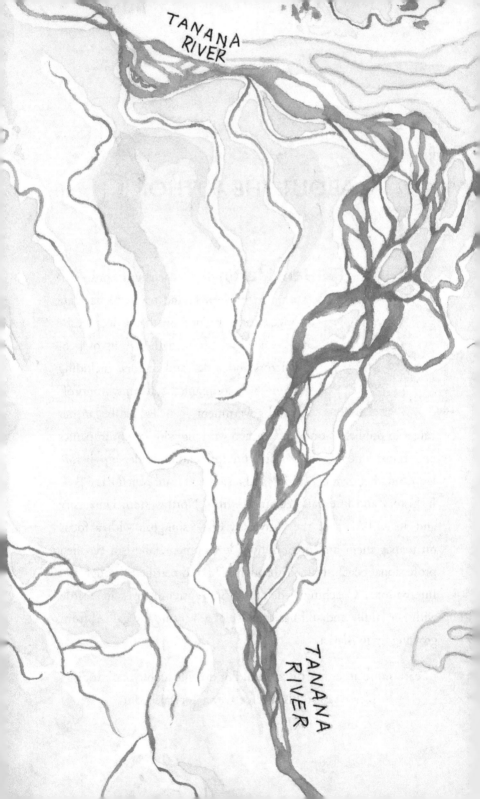

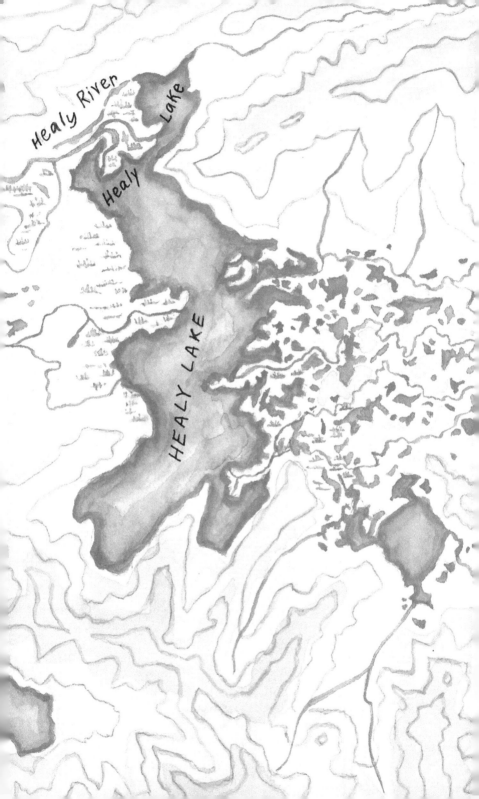